HUMAN CUISINE

HUMAN CUISINE

Copyright © 2008 by Ken Albala and Gary Allen
(except for the works of other contributors, who retain
all rights to their works)

All rights reserved. No part of this book may be
reproduced in any form, except brief excerpts for the
purpose of review, without written permission of the
authors.

Printed and distributed by Booksurge, a subsidiary of
Amazon.com.

Library of Congress Cataloging-in-Publication Data

Albala, Ken and Gary Allen, Editors
    Human Cuisine / Ken Albala and Gary Allen
    ISBN: 1-4196-9391-3

First printing, 2008
Printed in United States

MENU

Forewords (or Forewarned) — 1
Inviting Friends for Dinner 3
"Watch Out for My Uncle, He's a Cannibal!" 5

Aperitifs, Cocktails & Appetizers — 7
Forbidden Acts 9
Amuse Bouche 10
Recipes 17

The Pantry — 19
Cannibalism: Eat Right to Keep Fit 21
Fat Chance 23
Delicacy 43
The Watchman's Secret 50
Recipes 63

The Main Course — 65
Anti-Magellan 67
Mystery Meat: Curious Cases of Unintentional Cannibalism 79
Roast Fallopian Tubes 87
One Man's Muti... 92
The Economy of Food in Old New Guinea 101
Brain Food 109
Recipes 120

Something from the Oven — 124
Last Request 125
The Echo 130
Ribs 139
Kitchen Communion 154
Recipes 165

Just Desserts — 167
Friends for Dinner 169
Flouting the Taboo 177
The Human Remedy 187

Shrek, Enfant Terrible and Ex-Cannibal...*203*
Recipes..*206*

Coffee *&* Cordials   207

Grimma Gæst..*209*
The Eyes of Ghosts..*214*
Strangers in the Night...*218*
Recipes..*229*

The Kitchen Staff   230

Forewords (or Forewarned)

INVITING FRIENDS FOR DINNER

Ken Albala

"I believe that if ever I had to practice cannibalism, I might manage if there were enough tarragon around." James Beard

Written on a Placemat in a Pizzeria, in Verona, 29 June 2005

I have always had a strange fascination with human flesh. What does it taste like? How would an adventurous cook prepare it? Barbecued à la Arawak or braised in a Papuan *pot au feu*? Unwillingly, naturally, to cross the threshold of the criminal, I have had to make do with human by-products, such as a pleasant breast milk cheese reminiscent of chevre, or the end of my little pinkie accidentally lost in a pile of chopped onions after an accident. The possibilities seem endless when you begin to think about it. All sorts of human effluvia might become suitable ingredients. I have a Russian friend who drinks her own urine. I have seen many children relish a good chewy booger. Reputable chefs have tried cooking placenta. And think of all those tonsils and appendixes, gallbladders and who knows what just blithely tossed away. There must be more ways to serve human.

The idea for this collection came to me after hearing about a dinner designed by the Australian food writer Gay Bilson, in which she allegedly served black puddings made of her own blood. I actually had a pleasant conversation with her before realizing weeks later that she was the very same person that had planned that bloody repast. In any case, the idea stuck. What would happen if you asked food writers to write about cannibalism? My interest was really not in Hannibal Lecters or German internet cannibals, nor historical ritual man-eaters and those desperate tragedies in which people eat each other for survival. I wanted to initiate the discovery a human cuisine. Naturally, I turned to my pal Gary Allen first, and thus this book began to take form.

We agreed that we wanted to push the definition of cannibalism, subtly erasing the hard and fast line between horrid and everyday desires. We wanted to see if man eating could, under the right circumstances, be thinkable. There might even be ways we already practice cannibalism without considering it so, perhaps in medicines synthesized from human matter. If this collection might be accused of treading light-heartedly on a terrifying topic, it is only because there seems to be a little bit of cannibal in every person at some fundamental level. After all, those fortunate enough to have been breast-fed indulged in the most basic form of consuming the other. Even as adults, we "eat" each other in various sexual guises, playfully or literally. There is a good reason the language of food and sex overlap so seamlessly. Nor should we forget the practitioners of self-consumption—nail biters and such—nor even the most holy puss-sucking saint, like Catherine of Siena, whose seat in paradise was secured by her ingesting the suffering of the diseased.

As it turned out the volume contains much more than originally envisioned, with some frightening material too, that really turns my stomach. But there is just as much that straddles the line precisely between totally gross and titillating. It is all fascinating material, much of it fictional, some less so, and it does indeed reveal the capacity for cannibalism that lies in all of us.

Bon appetit.

"WATCH OUT FOR MY UNCLE, HE'S A CANNIBAL!"

Gary Allen

That's the way my nieces and nephews introduce me to their friends—oh wait, so does Ken Albala. I should probably point out that the ages of the children (not including my co-editor, who is a child only in the best metaphorical sense) range from eight to sixteen—those magical years when the ability to gross out one's friends is an important tool in achieving social status. It pleases me to me able to furnish a small *frisson* of disgust in order to aid in their quest for popularity.

I hasten to add that I am *not*, in fact, an anthropophagist.

I *have* read and written a lot about cannibals—enough, to be sure, to know that my interest in the consumption of human flesh is purely academic.

Mostly academic.

Well, *somewhat* academic.

There is a small, deeply buried part of me that is still (some people might argue that it's neither as small nor as deeply buried as I believe) adolescent. Let's just say I'm adolescent enough to enjoy watching the moment of transient fear and confusion that flickers across people's faces when they discover my obsession with cannibals. Most of them know of my interest in food and cooking—indeed, many of them have eaten meals I've prepared. In that brief darkening expression, one can almost see them counting off past dinners at my house, and wondering if they should have been more concerned about the identity of the main ingredients.

What I find curious, however, is that once their momentary social awkwardness passes, people who believed they knew nothing about such a disreputable subject start spouting little facts—and alleged facts—they've accumulated in normal life (perhaps when they, themselves, were adolescents). Sometimes they mention famous criminal cases, sometimes they repeat old clichés about encounters of explorers and missionaries with savage eaters of men, but most often they tell cannibal jokes.

There's something about the idea of munching on a nice leg o' man that makes everyone want to be a comedian.

Jokes are, in part, a way of hiding real anxiety about touchy subjects, but this is more than just nervous laughter; it's clear that these people *like* to discuss eating people—supposedly, the ultimate taboo—once someone else is kind enough to bring up the subject. William Bueller Seabrook, a man who acquired more first-hand knowledge about the fundamental facts of cannibalism than most of the *civilized* people who talk about it—including myself—wrote about cannibals in 1931, "Even aside from their delightful humorous aspect they are a highly interesting and wholly legitimate subject, whether for the adventurer or the learned anthropologist."

Cannibals *are* fascinating, and our fascination with them is, in itself… ummm, ahhhh… fascinating.

Of course, nothing interests us more than ourselves, and Ambrose Bierce, in an 1868 essay—*Did We Eat One Another?*—carried that rather obvious observation to its logical conclusion: "Our uniform vanity has given us the human mind as the acme of intelligence, the human face and figure as the standard of beauty. Of course we cannot deny to human fat and lean an equal superiority over beef, mutton and pork."

This little collection does not aim to resolve the question of the superiority of human fat and lean over beef, mutton and pork, or whether humans should, or should not, be on the menu—but I like to think that some of the tales here will add appreciably to the range of topics available for *discussion* over dinner.

If such talk puts others off their feed, so be it—it just means that there will all the more leftovers for us.

APERITIFS, COCKTAILS & APPETIZERS

"Humans are the only animals that have children on purpose with the exception of guppies, who like to eat theirs."
P.J. O'Rourke

"Man is the only animal that can remain on friendly terms with the victims he intends to eat until he eats them."
Samuel Butler

FORBIDDEN ACTS

Tamara Watson

My overwhelming desire is
to bite the dentist as his gloved
hand approaches my mouth
it seems, cautiously, even timidly.

I could always say biting
was an involuntary action,
like blinking, or accidental,
like shooting a loved one
you mistake for a burglar.

Today, another child took a gun
to school. He could not state
a reason for having the gun
or for using it. It just happened,
like I might bite the dentist.

If I bit the dentist, I would not be able
to say why I did it. I could describe
the sensation of his fingers caught
between my oversized, numbed teeth.
No one would hold me responsible.

The child, numbed by indifference,
does not feel responsibility.
I decide not to bite the dentist. Not
Today. The child decides to shoot.
It could be the only difference.

AMUSE BOUCHE
Riva Soucie

Marion eats what she is.

Her energy worker says she's punishing herself.

"She's right," Marion supposes, "But I never cut myself. Too scared or too squeamish, I guess." She draws blood, it's true, but perhaps those times are aberrations of a sort.

At times, she thinks it's just a habit. For a number of years, she tried replacing it. First with beer. Then light rum, cheap wine, and strong weed. But the side effects were killing her in bits, so she gave them all up.

Gave them up for something much more covert, but just as effective.

"I use my teeth to tear my nails and the skin around them, swallowing tiny pieces of my body. Until my fingertips and nail beds are shredded, beaten, and bleeding," she admits to her therapist, the licensed psychologist that Peter, her fiancé, had found for her. He was suspicious of Marion's involvement with her energy worker, even though Marion had explained that it was just another word for hypnotist. But this had only fueled Peter's discomfort. He felt that all that talk of emotions and *spirituality*, for God's sake, filled Marion's head full of hocus pocus. And until the therapist got her straightened out, he forbade her to eat in front of him.

The therapist suggests that Marion might be obsessive-compulsive. She lists Marion's compulsions: counting, ordering, tracing, throwing away, preparing, listing, planning, cleaning, and reading and reviewing. And, she adds, nail biting could easily be added to the list.

"Perhaps," Marion thinks, but doesn't say out loud, "although, unlike the other compulsions, the counting and the rest, I have control over eating myself. I could stop anytime."

Maybe she doesn't want to.

She finds her appetite steady and insistent. She peels and sometimes uses scissors or nail clippers to cut small strips of skin, nail, and blemishes from several places on her body. Her choices are calculated, and she eats the pieces dutifully. The crunch of a nail or several layers of skin between Marion's teeth sickens Peter whenever he happens to be in the room.

She prefers eating alone anyway.

Maybe Marion's therapist is right. Her anxiety *is* temporarily relieved by the feel of her own skin between her lips and teeth, and by the bits of flesh as they travel down her throat. "Maybe I need medication," she thinks, and wrinkles her nose. "Or, at least more therapy. After all, who likes the taste and feel of her own flesh? It must be a disorder." The thought shocks Marion. Shocks her and makes her anxious.

So, she starts eating, and soon she is comforted by the pain that seeps into the tips of her fingers. But, she wakes up in the night because she has knocked her throbbing thumb against something hard. "What *was* that?" she wonders. She runs her hands over her comforter in the dark, realizing guiltily that she's hit her thumb only on the blankets. She brings it to her lip and feels that it is hot and swollen. Starting now to get really pissed off at herself, she hopes it isn't infected.

—

The calm she feels after eating herself is only temporary. It is always followed by feelings of blame, shame, stupidity, and guilt, and so she punishes herself again: scratching at the tiny bumps on the backs of her arms until they bleed, swallowing the bits that come off. Or, ripping off her cuticles one by one, sinking her front teeth into the jellied inner layers of the soft tissue around her fingernails.

This is why her energy worker is trying to help her remember exactly what she's punishing herself for. "I hate to break it to her," Marion thinks ruefully, "but it's not going to come in a flash of light. I don't eat because I've done something bad in the *past*. Look at me *now*, for God's sake. I procrastinate. I swallow my words and let people push me around. I don't exercise or floss my teeth."

"It doesn't take hypnosis for me to go back in my childhood," Marion tells her.

"In my family, bodily functions were a source of immense personal pride. What you left in the toilet was always table talk at dinner. But, even to my parents, who were, ah…a bit on the unconventional side…"

"What do you mean by *unconventional?*" the energy worker asks kindly as she gently pats the back of Marion's hand.

"Well, for one thing, in the 80s they stocked up on ten-gallon sealed containers of wheat, rye, and buckwheat. This was so we would survive either the event of a total infrastructure breakdown or the coming of Christ, both of which were imminent, they were sure, and both in which I lived in total fear for twenty years."

Marion laughs out loud at this. "Now that's a reason to repress childhood memories" she smiles ruefully.

"So, even though they were unconventional, they were fairly militant, too. And, they could *not* tolerate a daughter who ate her own nails and skin so…violently. And seemingly, with such elation! My mother tried desperately to get me to quit. She threatened, bribed me with money, toys, and manicures, bought me bitter-tasting polish, and recently, has simply reverted to ordering me to stop. All these tactics have only made it feel all the better to eat, though."

"Why do you think that is?"

"Well, when I'm not in control, I get anxious. When I eat, I have power. I'm in control.

"Like when I eat from my heels and the balls of my toes, I use nail clippers to pinch off several layers of skin; lots of times, the cuts run too deep and I'm pulling on pieces of flesh that just aren't supposed to come off my body. But, I am disciplined. I am in control. I make my own rules. If I hurt myself, I am tough.

I pile the scraps of dry skin, sometimes attached to pieces of live flesh, on the rug. The pile is order and it is product."

Later that day, after clipping and pulling, Marion examines her collection, picking one of the pieces up and trying it between her teeth. It surprises her, as eating herself always does, with its simplicity. Soothes her with its lack of demand. She crunches through it delightedly and swallows.

Whenever she runs out of free edges on her nails, Marion inevitably turns to the spongy writing callus on her left ring finger. First, she trims the edges, concentrating on the top layer of deadish skin, and then plunges deeper into the nerve-dense flesh. This hurts like fire, and brings quick relief. It's a bit of an adrenalin rush, her body releasing feel-good chemicals like mad, trying to counteract the pain.

She eats the rest of it standing up in front of the patio doors.

The skin underneath the callus is ragged because it doesn't come off cleanly. It is sore and mushy and an angry red color now, but Marion becomes obsessed with the task of cleaning up the raw edges with her teeth. She works on it for a few minutes, testing how much peeling can be done by feeling the terrain of the skin with the sensitive end of her tongue. Finally, the knuckle begins to sag and bleed. She's disgusted at the callus for giving in so easily, and she feels pleased that she's destroyed it.

"Can't eating myself be just a bit fun, too?" Marion asks her therapist insolently.

"I mean it isn't all about stress and fear and dark places, is it? Maybe I just like to experiment. You know, enjoy myself."

"Like at summer camp when I was ten, to prove my virility, I suppose, I picked at a scab on my knee, got a tiny piece of dried blood stuck to a wispy bit of dead skin, and tried it between my front teeth. It wasn't bad. Dry. And, a little bit salty. I watched the blood bead around the new gap in my wound and used it to paint a six-pointed star on my knee.

Or, when I was seven, and I accidentally peed a little when I was playing outside. I went inside to change, but as I was taking off my underwear, I noticed the wet spot on the cotton crotch, and stuck the very tip of my tongue on it to see what it tasted like. Immediately censoring myself, I stuck exactly the same amount of my tongue in my mother's powder compact. Apparently that was the substance I thought most able to obliterate organic matter."

—

"I'm made of meat, after all, aren't I?" Marion thinks in the shower the next morning.

"Who better to eat, than myself? I don't eat beef or pork, so maybe I'm trolling for iron or protein. At least I know that I was raised somewhat humanely. Could be that I'm fed up with choice and pressure and fear, and that I just want a little time alone with my thoughts. Non-regulated. Simple. Pressure-free. Just me."

The hot water stings the raw ends of her fingers. When she gets out, she splays them in the air, inspecting her work. Ten rubbery-looking, ragged nubs of bone stretched over with skin. She sighs. They're troublesome, like yesterday's polluted virgin. She has overindulged.

She dries her hands brusquely; when they're damp and mutilated like this, they offend her. She's suddenly cold, and she guards the rest of her body. "Who knows how far I'll go?" she thinks glumly.

At that thought, she feels exquisite.

The violent meter of the meal she ate last night has sustained her even through the night. She feels deliciously beaten, and so she surrenders. This is soothing. It was worth it then.

Marion sighs again, this time in contentment.

—

On the bus to Peter's, she tries not to put her hands in her mouth. It's her rule when she's in public. She has a seat though, so her hands are free, and she can't resist.

"I'll just fix that little hangnail on my thumb," she promises herself, but bites too far, and the skin opens reluctantly. She reasons that she should peel it off so it doesn't get torn later. Halfway through the motion, she has to steel herself as it begins to bleed, but she needs to finish. She swallows the skin quickly and sucks the side of her thumb to contain the blood.

"This eating business is a solid thing," she thinks hungrily, "my thing, my shaky soma: the body made of bread and jelly, and it's a hungry debauchee: the seducer, the friend."

She wraps the bottom of her t-shirt around her thumb and sits on her hands the rest of the way to Peter's.

When she arrives, her thumb is still bleeding, and an elusive ledge of skin hangs at the base of the nail.

"He's going to lecture me," she thinks resentfully, "I know it. He finds my snacking objectionable."

She gingerly tucks her thumb into her fist and raises the other hand to knock.

When he comes to the door, he's distracted though, so she waves her thumb quietly and gleefully around the kitchen, watching the blood pool and sucking it lollypop-style. The metallic taste of the blood, which is fascinating and familiar, stops too quickly.

Usually, with Peter, Marion is one part confessional and two parts apology, but she doesn't feel apologetic today. She feels tight and dark: a puckered navel. Yes, that's it. She is a knot with no way to explain itself, but one that is also secretly pleased for being so self-contained.

By morning, Marion can't take Peter's moral high-grounding a moment longer, and she hides under the covers to lay into her fingertips. While she's under there, she gets really lewd, swallowing some of the dry mucus that's stuck in her eyes.

Peter pokes his head under the sheet, and catches her, knowing. Demanding an explanation, an apology, his face gets red and his forehead gets really shiny. Marion giggles a little, thinking about how much he looks like a split-open tomato.

"Peter," she begins, as if speaking to a little child, "eating myself makes me feel less *pastiche* for a moment, yes. But, the feeling is a flash in the pan. Soon, I feel made up again, put together like a bad suit. So, I pick at the seams, pull loose threads, unravel what might not even be there at all. And, every time I go too deep, pull too hard, I vow to swear it off. But, many an overeater has made solemn promises following a binge.

I love to eat what I am."

RECIPES

Dr. Scholl's Confit (Toe Jam)
Select a dozen of the gnarliest, most fetid, toes you can find—with corns, athlete's foot fungus and anything else that smells like stinky cheese. Put these in a pot with a gallon of water and boil vigorously for five hours. Gently pick the meat from the bones and return to the pot. The collagen in the bones will help the jam set. Keep in the fridge until ready to use, and spread on toast points as a dainty appetizer.

Ken Albala

Promethean Foie Gras
Trick one of your colleagues into giving away some corporate secret. This is certain to incur the wrath of the CEO, who will hang the silly goose out to dry in some god-forsaken spot. Almost immediately, human resources, a flock of ravenous lawyers, and assorted other corporate birds of prey will gather to divide up the poor fellow's liver. Collect any leftover scraps, warm gently over some stolen fire, and serve on toasted pita points. Don't worry about running out—there will always be more tomorrow.

Gary Allen

Occhi di Santa Lucia
On the longest night of the year, buy a plane ticket to Syracuse. Sicily or New York will do. Find a virgin to persecute. First burn her, to no avail. She is miraculously restored. Then have her eyes plucked out. She will serve her eyes herself, two per plate. A few drops of lemon juice and a dash of Tabasco is all that's needed. Slurp them down one by one. Then start singing.

Ken Albala

THE PANTRY

"Cannibal: A gastronome of the old school who preserves the simple tastes and adheres to the natural diet of the pre-pork period."
Ambrose Bierce, *The Devil's Dictionary*

CANNIBALISM: EAT RIGHT TO KEEP FIT

Laurel Massé

A few years ago I apprenticed to an herbalist. She was a follower of Tom Brown, "The Tracker," who had taught her impeccable wilderness survival skills and imbued her with his apocalyptic vision of the end times. "The red skies," she called those final days, and they were constantly on her mind. "When the red skies come," she warned, "you'll have to eat your dogs." I shuddered, but my then-husband, member of a supremely dysfunctional Italian family, said, "Tell her we'll be eating my fat relatives first."

I have no doubt that I could, if it was absolutely necessary for my survival, eat my dogs. I cannot however imagine a situation in which they would not be more helpful to me alive. Could I run down a deer? The energy expenditure for me might prove too costly. But for a Belgian Sheepdog, whose breed standard is "always in motion except when under command?" Playtime. And am I alert to every sound, can I defend myself as well as their teeth can defend me?

The overweight relatives, however, would be too calorically expensive to feed and relatively easy to capture. So what would stop me from eating Barbara? She tips the scales at over 285 pounds. I would be able to feed my tribe quite well. And Joanne's not much smaller and a whole lot more trouble. It's so practical. Rid myself of a nuisance, keep starvation at bay, make the world a better place by breaking a chain of family cruelty—sooner or later after the catastrophe we'd repopulate, and don't we want to world to be better? So why is the idea abhorrent?

It is because I know their bloodlines and I know what they eat. They smoke. They drink. They eat sugar by the ton. The family is riddled with cancer, which is ugly foul flesh that looks and smells "wrong." There is diabetes. There is emphysema. This can't be healthy flesh to eat.

What about my blood sister? She is fit, strong, health-conscious—acceptable fare—and a member of my blood tribe. If I did accept that it would be right to eat my sister, then fairness dictates that she could—if I died, or if she could catch me—eat me. Intellectually this seems fine, like organ donor cards. But has anybody poor ever signed those cards without wondering if the day would come when somebody rich would need a kidney and a surgeon would come knocking at the door or a car "accident" would magically happen? Some researchers have suggested that people respond differently to the idea of cannibalism based on whether they are what one writer called "intellectually adventurous" or "students with little or no academic background." I believe this difference has nothing to do with intellect and everything to do with perceived powerlessness in the latter group. After all, which economic group is it that ends up with no academic background? This is a world wherein Keith Richards can stay on heroin as long as he wants because he can afford to go to Switzerland to have his blood "washed" or replaced with someone else's. Is that going to be available to the average reader of *People* or *Rolling Stone* anytime soon? Or to any junkie in the South Bronx? Perhaps it's not the idea of people eating people that is disturbing but the certainty that you will be the one on the plate, with someone like Rupert Murdoch or Ken Lay wielding the carving knife, in a logical conclusion of capitalism.

My health-food sister is of my tribe, by love and by blood. The only way I could eat her, or she, me, is if she and I together designed a ritual to be enacted on that occasion, a way of commemorating the life that is gone, and sanctifying the life that will continue because of it. It would have to include a celebration of the consciousness of the one who is to be consumed. And it would have to be undertaken as solemnly as the Mass, for that is what it would be. Not hunter and prey, but rather communion and loving agreement about the sanctity of human life.

My former in-laws would never imagine themselves as prey. That's how I could catch them. But eat them? There is not enough connection, and not enough love.

FAT CHANCE

Ken Albala & Lisa Cooperman

Surinder Singh, whose friends called him Suri, stepped into the waiting room of his cosmetic surgery clinic. Not a single patient. The magazines lay unruffled, the cool air unperfumed by visitors. One woman had arrived that morning to inquire about "silhouette reduction" procedures. She knew that Dr. Singh worked on celebrities—singers, actors, even a successful basketball player who was able to postpone retirement after having a few pounds surgically removed. She left with some generalized promises and a packet of information, more worried and uncertain than when she arrived. But Dr. Singh was used to inquiries like this.

The office and waiting area were bright and tidy, minimal and tasteful but not antiseptic, as was the doctor himself. Hours of expensive consultation had gone into the design of his surgical suite, which had in turn led to an overhaul of the doctor's wardrobe. He hoped that his new narrow trousers and the indefinable non-color of his neatly pressed shirt belied the confidence his well-heeled clients placed in him, but now he was not so sure. At one time Suri could have anticipated a packed waiting room every morning. He never left the office before nine; his long days spent assuring alarmingly younger women, and men too, about the safety of liposuction since various breakthroughs in the mid 80s. "Your recovery will be swift and relatively pain-free. Liposuction cannot replace a healthy diet and moderate exercise, but it can dramatically enhance your appearance and boost your self-confidence." At this point in the flow of soothing patter he would glance over his shoulder at the certificate on the wall from the American Plastic Surgeons Association, the gold standard of those who worked on the perpetually perfect. A circumspect eye might catch discreet testimonials from well-known celebrities.

He explained that a tiny stainless steel tube called a micro-cannula simply draws out the excess fat by means of a gentle but efficient vacuum. Scarring is minimal, and normally only local anesthesia was required. Suri was able to launch into this sales pitch at a moment's notice with the perfect timbre of reassurance and carefully modulated promise. But this afternoon his office was empty. His secretary was idly searching the internet for cheap apartments in Los Feliz. His nurse-assistant was nowhere to be found.

Suri blamed the lull in business on the Atkins craze. More people were cutting carbs, finding it cheaper and less threatening than surgery. Yet he was sure the tide would change soon, just as it has after every other diet fad had swept the nation and failed. He was sure the pasta contingent would launch such a successful counter attack, that people would once again crave starch. Soon they would be raiding the bread aisles, stuffing bagels and donuts down their throats, packing on the pounds and whimpering at his doors for help.

For the moment, though, there was nothing he could do but daydream. For some reason the waiting room looked cleaner and more sterile than usual. The absence of fat bodies on the oyster nubuck couches deprived the space of its usual fug of body odor and tension. Today it was quiet, too cold, and smelled strongly of fake lemon disinfectant. Suri turned on a square-toed shoe and stepped into the operating room, eyeing the surgical steel counter, the precisely arranged suction tubes, the rows of hypodermic needles and tiny vials of anti-inflammatory medicines. The room gleamed with rows metal tanks, miles of tubing and odd pumps that gurgled and spurted like whipped cream canisters. But the operating table was empty. No one being prepped, no impatient nurse or anxious mother trying to catch a glimpse hovered nearby. No one.

Suri wondered whether his parents would still be as proud of him now as they had been on the day he first opened his practice. They had brought him from Calcutta as a boy, encouraged his studies and eventually saw him graduate with honors from medical school. His specialty was surgery, although not the sort they had expected—cosmetic surgery—but surgery all the same. And their son worked on some of the biggest names in Hollywood. Of course client confidentiality prevented him from pointing smugly to the faces and bottoms that he had worked on when they watched TV together in their south county apartment. Nonetheless he did drop hints. And his parents played along "Oh my, what lovely thighs. Do you think she looks thinner? Maybe our Suri sculpted those!" Not that being thin mattered to them in the least. In fact, fat was a sign of health in his family. Heaven forefend he ever bring home an emaciated woman, his mother would fatten her up quick enough, plying her with samosas and fried pappadams the moment he presented her bony butt at the door. In any case—and despite years of enduring distant relatives who had cousins, who had daughters—Suri had never yet brought home a woman of any kind.

He was proud of his position in the medical community, although he suspected that his success had something to do with the perception that he was an outsider, someone who would not gossip, because the fundamental racism of Hollywood ensured that he would never have someone of "significance" with whom to gossip. Still, he was essentially happy with the choices he had made in life. He was single, but imagined someday settling down with the right woman and starting a family. But today he was too busy thinking of the alarming dearth of clients of girth. Distractedly, he settled into the leather armchair behind his desk, rifled through a drawer stuffed with miscellaneous papers and produced a rumpled half-eaten bag of potato chips. This was his only true weakness in life, he thought as he sunk his teeth into a salty, greasy, oversized chip and savored the malicious crunching noise as it reverberated through his skull.

Ruth was not about to be chastised yet another day. Yesterday was an absolute disaster. For the briefest second, she had turned her head felt the steel slice cleanly through the very tip of her knuckle as she carefully, and properly, held down a peeled potato with her left hand. "No big deal" she insisted as she scrounged around for a band-aid. It wasn't a big deal. Everyone gets cut in a working kitchen. But greater damage had been done. Some errant drops of crimson blood had trickled into the stockpot immediately to the left of her workstation, and a few perched on the rim. More importantly, the flap of knuckle skin was missing. Had she waved her hands about to accomplish this? Inside the pot, a day's batch of demi-glace had been simmering at the lowest possible setting since about five that morning. If no one had seen it she could have assured herself that a few drops of blood in the stock, well cooked, would never hurt anyone. Blood and far worse found its way onto every plate in some form or another. Of course everyone in the kitchen knew exactly what happened to Ruth's knuckle skin.

Under ordinary circumstances it would have been back to business as usual, but a health inspector had been there the week before and gave the restaurant a "satisfactory with warning" certificate. It didn't mean that business ground to a halt; in fact customers never even saw the certificates unless they specifically asked. The kitchen had been just a bit too messy and dirty for the inspector's taste. He told them to clean up their act or next time things would be different, by which he meant worse, of course.

So at 4:30 on a Thursday afternoon there stood the chef, a squat Serbian bull of a man, with one thick eyebrow across his forehead and a harvest of waxy excrescences sprouting across his face, peering into the fathomless depths of the 20-quart stockpot. Today he was not about to overlook a stray cabbage leaf on the floor, let alone a spattering of human blood. "RRROOOTH!!! Zese people have a way of showink up unhexpected. Maybe ze day hafter a warnink." His face was turning red, and it looked like he might burst a vein in his neck.

Ruth was beside herself. Just two days ago she messed up a scallop mousseline foam. She had the gas cartridge set in properly, the pump nozzle was clean and primed. But instead of a fluffy white Ferran Adriàesque mound of evanescent shellfish laced with essence of lemon grass, a thin viscous liquid dribbled from the nozzle. What could have gone wrong? Why did it deflate? So the cut was strike two, and she began to seriously doubt whether she was really sous-chef material after all.

They made it through the night. A sudden change in menu. The duck leg confit in a fig marmalade reduction (which depended on the demi-glace) was sadly unavailable. The waiters offered the pathetic explanation that there were no fresh figs to be had in the market that morning. It was frankly humiliating for Ruth, knowing that everyone in the restaurant had to lie to cover up her stupid mistake. A quarter of a millimeter slip.

She got home that night close to two. Famished as usual, and dove into her normal routine of late-night grazing. She didn't subsist solely on junk food; sometimes she had crackers and cheese, some cold cuts, a stray vegetable. Anything as long as it didn't have to be cooked. The strain of cooking for hours on end would not allow her to set foot anywhere near a pan. And if that meant ripping open a bag of chips, all the better. They were, in fact, the most satisfying things imaginable to her in moments like these. There was something primal about biting down on something too big for your mouth, and hearing teeth shatter crisp sheets of starch. It was if this satisfied some basic hard-wired instinct to hear food, which our ancestors learned to appreciate directly as they gnawed though bones leaving us with the same desire without really knowing why. A displaced instinct for destruction satisfied with snacking.

Ruth was an inveterate snacker. She was not exactly fat, a few lumpy bits here and there, some cellulite, but it wasn't something she ever considered terribly important. After all, she had aspirations of being a great chef someday. Who would trust a thin chef? After an hour's disconsolate nibbling she switched on the TV in her small dank apartment, flipped through channels for a minute and stopped for no particular reason to gaze at one of the strangest looking faces she had ever seen.

There sat behind cheap particle board desk in a too small suit an elderly man with a shock of thick grey hair combed first up then back, a generous application of pomade apparently lacquering the tsunami into place. On his upper lip a prodigious growth of whiskers suggested the presence of a hairy old rat that had nested there one day and taken up permanent residence. He was also slightly cross-eyed and unfocused, making him look like an aging Friedrich Nietzsche, though maybe without the syphilis. An extremely unlikely prophet, but that's what he appeared to be. Or perhaps it was Jim Morrison returned from hiding after 30 years.

As he was speaking he flailed his arms about, gazing about the room, and ranting about chakras, celestial unguents coursing through invisible medians on the body, orthogenic qi, and living in harmony with the ambrosial cosmos.

Rubbish, thought Ruth, about to switch it off. She assumed any moment he would start plugging his miracle weight loss yoga video, or his super Krishna consciousness fat buster with ephedra. That's all that was on TV this late at night. But the message was nothing of the sort. In fact, the lunatic on the screen seemed to have been praising obesity. "Fat connects us to the world soul" "Resist the hucksters and pill pushers who tell you a pure spirit resides in a miniscule waistline and six-pack abs." At least that's what she thought he was saying. The guy was pretty fat himself, and so were the women who flitted in and out of the picture around him like white trash dakinis. She thought that any second these "before" shots would cut to the "after" and the smiling bikini-clad housewives would be commence playing volleyball on the beach.

But it never happened. The guy began to quote scriptures. Jesus was a lover of feasts. Think of the miracles he performed: loaves of bread miraculously appear (yes, Jesus ate carbs) and wine flows endlessly from bottomless jugs. Fishes offer themselves to be caught. The ancient Brahmins were no different. At first they were great eaters of meat. Even beef. Yahweh demanded that the Israelites burn the fat and entrails of their sacrifices on the altar, and he would smell the smoke; apparently barbecue pleased him exceedingly. Krishna was nourished with ghee, the Buddha grew fat and found his greatest moments of solace rubbing his portentous belly. Zeus ate ambrosia, Thor competed in heroic bouts of eating and drinking. In every religion, the celestial beings eat, grow happy and fat.

Priests had merely invented the idea of dieting because they knew in their hearts that they could never be like the Gods. In their spite they made a virtue of starvation. Bodily mortification became the path to so-called eternal life. No food, no sex, no pleasure of any kind. No violence either. The very things that had given us success as a species now became suspect. They made up stories about Jesus fasting in the desert for forty days. They invented vegetarianism from Brahmins, because they knew the masses of lower castes would rise up and kill them when they were the only ones eating beef. The Gods' original plan for us—to live in the land of milk and honey and flourish on the fat of the land—was inverted to serve their all-consuming desire to dominate.

Ruth had enough by this point. Whether it was exhaustion or a sudden twinge of guilt over having eaten the entire bag of chips that now made her feel like a Bodhisattva, she decided to attempt sleep. And pray that tomorrow would be better. No knife accidents, no deflated foams, No. ...she was already asleep.

—

Weeks passed at the restaurant. There were other accidents. Not hers, at least not most of them, though today she did cut herself a few times. The inspector did return. He sauntered into the kitchen, ceremoniously snapped a latex glove onto his left hand as if readying himself for a proctology exam, bent down and wiped his hand beneath a shelf of flour and spices. Of course the space had been cleaned. Two or three times. Nothing to worry about thought chef Banac. Until the needle-nosed inspector lifted himself from the floor with his gloved hand aloft, brandishing what appeared to be a raisin.

"No! It can't be, thought Banac. Please Got in Heaven!" But it was indeed exactly what they feared the most. A tiny, petrified football shaped rat turd.

The new certificate read "Temporary Suspension" and was prominently displayed on the front door. If a warning wouldn't do, a loss of revenue would make any restaurant clean up shop. They were still open, but customers stopped coming. The rumors spread. Aerated foams and concentrated reductions notwithstanding, Chez Ivo was going down the tubes. And fast. Ruth and all the others could see the writing on the wall. Restaurants rarely lasted five years in this town anyway, but with a death sentence like this they would be closed within a few weeks. Bills unpaid, shipments halted, menu slashed, busboys laid off. It was inevitable. Within a few more days the restaurant was practically gone.

Banac opened a bottle of slivovitz after turning out the marquee light at the front of the restaurant. The few stores left in the kitchen had been divided up between the kitchen and wait staff, and the gear was stacked unsteadily near the back door. He had a cousin with a truck and a spacious garage, no sense letting the bank get his entire life savings. Ruth fidgeted while he rummaged through a pile of papers for her letter of recommendation, his glass sloshing here and there. Apparently he had already finished a few and was hoping to convince Ruth to share another. Palming the damp letter she tried to edge backwards toward her car and away from the craziness of her career choice but his plum-colored eyes stopped her. "You know, Roooth, you haf ze makings of good chef, you haf a special feel for cracklink, so crisp." Groping for a tumbler and pouring her a glassful "but as sous-chef you har no good, you, you must fry." With these words she tossed back the acrid liquid and Banac immediately filled it again.

Late that night Ruth's peeling LeBaron pulled into the parking lot of parallel spaces at a pronounced diagonal. The all-night grocery was an island of light and the friendly Vietnamese men who worked there, acolytes in the temple of convenience food. So many choices.

Moments later Suri's charcoal gray Lexus also pulled up. Both Suri and Ruth headed in exactly the same direction just seconds apart; Suri walking with purpose in broad measured steps, Ruth careening somewhat from the booze. Time seemed to move slowly, as it often does under preternatural light, probably the effect of squinting and the pressure exerted on the brain as it recoils from the barrage of offensive packages and assailing odors.

His hand reached for a bag of reduced-fat all-natural chips with ridges, way on the bottom shelf, and a second later another hand groped in the same space. "Oops, sorry" she said, already closer than a sober person would ever get. "No problem," said Suri instantly recognizing the woman who had come into his office a few weeks before asking about procedures. But this time he noticed her, that is, the woman, not the patient—especially her luxuriant red curls and the curve of her hips. Anxious not to appear as if he recognized her—doctors do not associate with patients—he did something very silly in desperation. By this point Ruth had already purloined the bag of chips, apparently the last of its kind on the shelf, but was still crouched low with it, balancing precariously beside the bottom shelf.

Even the slightest push would have put Ruth on her butt, and that really was not Suri's intention, but when he grabbed the bag out of her hands, yelled "fumble" and began to make a mad dash for the end zone, he noticed that she had already toppled, and was already giggling wildly. Naturally he apologized profusely, fawningly and helped her up. Without asking he opened the bag of chips and offered them as a peace gesture. She was still giggling. And it was infectious.

Even though she already knew what he did, by reflex she asked anyway. "Oh, a surgeon, cosmetic." Both pretended that they had never met. He then noticed her bandaged fingers and felt obligated to say something now that he admitted his profession. "Is that ok, would you like me to look at it?" "Oh, no, It's fine, just another one of my minor run-ins with sharp cutlery. Knife accident last week. It happens all the time. I'm a chef, er—sous chef. Or at least was until the restaurant closed."

"What restaurant?" "Chez Ivo—do you know it? It's on…was on…" "Of course, I've been there a few times. Pretty good. A little pretentious, shellfish foams and such." "Oh, yes I've been at that station one too many times" "So, what happened, it's closing?" "Closed—bad inspections, dirt and such..." she said while trying to hide her wounded hand. Suri had a hard time not wincing at the thought of all the dirt he'd eaten there. "Really it wasn't that dirty, no worse that anywhere else, we just got an inspector with a mean streak. Maybe someone never paid him off."

"Oh, I'm really sorry about all this. Do you have another job?" he asked. "Nope, nothing yet. I'm going to be living on these for a while" as she brandished a ridged chip on high. "Well, you know, I just happen to be looking for some help at the clinic. It doesn't need to be long term, just until you find another restaurant job. As he said it, he wondered what could have made him offer a job so compulsively.

Wow, she said, "I'm good with a knife. Well, not really." He stopped her, "No... no surgical procedures involved. I'd have you maintain the files, order equipment and deal with the vendors. Things I end up doing, but really shouldn't be wasting time on—that didn't come out right—you know, I need an office manager. Not to answer phones or greet clients, but to maintain the books and such." With few other options and unwilling to show her face once again at the temp agency, she said yes. And that was that.

She started work about a week later. She was given minor tasks at first. None of which she performed particularly well, but her presence in the clinic made everything seem brighter and cheerier. Clients who came in an expected to see buff little nurses touting the procedure found a slightly heavy woman with sympathetic eyes. Someone they trusted. It reassured them that they would be alright, and that the surgery would not change their lives overnight, and that was ok. No one could be perfect, and Ruth reminded them that it really didn't matter. Self-image was everything. And to tell the truth, Ruth liked it there. She began to grow very fond of Suri. She spent more time attending to his personal needs than to the office. And he never told her to do otherwise.

Remarkably, the business started to flourish again. Some old clients returned for another job. A few new celebrities showed up. Suri was back in the swing of business. And he believed it was Ruth that turned his fortune around.

Ruth meanwhile took careful account of the comings and goings of the office. As best she could. There were boxes with clean new knives, tubes and bandages, shining canisters of fat lining the back porch to be picked up by a biohazard truck. Then there were bills and bills and more bills. Insurance companies to deal with, inevitably refusing to pay claims despite their stated policies. There were calls from customers wondering how long to keep their tight bandages on. Of course she had no competence answering any of these questions. She was much better fetching coffee or snacks for Suri.

After a few weeks it became obvious to everyone that she was totally superfluous in the clinic. And she began to get in the way once business really picked up. She accidentally misinformed one customer about post-operative drugs. She switched records of two patients by mistake. This was the stuff of lawsuits. Suri knew he had to find something else for Ruth to do before she ruined him. As much as he loved having her around, to catch a faint whiff of her sweet-smelling soap as she turned the corner, to see her smile widely for no particular reason. These things were magic. But her energies were totally misdirected. She needed a kitchen to focus that power and talent.

Suri then came up with yet another audacious scheme. He would do everything to keep her around, but he knew an office romance was just as bad as a client romance. He needed her at home. Perhaps she never really admitted to herself that he was falling in love with her. Or she denied that it was even possible for this successful, thin and neat Indian man to fall in love with a fat woman. But it did happen, and she was tacitly complicit. Which is exactly why she agreed to this plan.

She would open her own restaurant. Perhaps just a cafe at first, a small unpretentious place. She would run the cafe and he would be the silent backer. No strings attached. She could do things however she saw fit, and he would earn money on his investment. Even if it didn't turn a profit at first, Ruth's happiness was actually his first concern, and he told her so.

Whether it was lack of confidence or unwillingness to deal with surly customers and undependable staff, she balked at the idea of a cafe. No more restaurants. She realized her real passion was cooking, not organizing dining experiences. Why not a small business? He could put up the money for a small industrial space, finance the equipment and all the supplies and she would work on her own. Someplace nearby so she could visit the clinic often and zoned for a bakery or something like that. No retail space. No customers' faces or counting change. She would sell to other retailers, market her product broadly and spend most of her time in the kitchen where she wanted to be. No boss was the most important part. Just an indulgent silent partner to finance the budding business.

But what to make? She considered various options. Cookies? Market saturated. Pastries? Too perishable and fragile. You need a shop to sell baked goods anyway. Candies maybe. No, all controlled by the big manufacturers. She settled on chips. Why not? Sure there were gourmet brands. Kettle chips, Terra chips with funky tropical tubers. But no local brands making small batches. And no one selling chips flavored with truly gourmet ingredients. We're not talking sea salt, cracked black pepper or parmesan cheese. Those were all mass-produced chemically-enhanced flavors anyway. She was thinking of truffles and chevre, foie gras with poached pear, enoki mushroom with organic free-range quail. Why not? They sold hedgehog chips in Britain, chicken flavor in Australia—and those were dreadful. But with fresh ingredients and freshly made batches, she could virtually invent the gourmet chip. It would be the highest end of a very low-brow market; the ultimate marriage of junk food and haute cuisine. Selling for ten bucks a bag, only the lavish and profligate would truly understand.

The business started very well. Huge frying vats were installed. A super-speed potato peeler and slicer. An electronic fire alarm and sprinkler system, hydraulic vents. There were state of the art refrigerators, a small loading platform once she needed truckloads of fresh potatoes and veggies. Storage closets everywhere. It was a fantastic working space.

At first she had some trouble with frying temperatures. Not only had she never actually made a chip before, but certainly never on this scale. Some of the ingredients burned before the potatoes cooked. Others turned soggy after ten minutes out of the fryer. The recipes needed serious tweaking. What recipes? She was making this up as she went along. Then there was the problem of the right oil. Some went rancid quickly. Some had too low a smoking point. Olive oil would have been great otherwise. Some were too expensive, like peanut oil. She toyed briefly with the idea of vegetable shortening. Infinite shelf life, cheap. The industrial manuals preferred it. Cheap canola was a better option, but no flavor whatsoever. Safflower was worse. She even thought of olestra, but what kind of niche could a non-fat gourmet chip hope to capture? Too much. If you eat foie gras, damn it, you probably don't care what fat your chips are fried in. After reading Jeffrey Steingarten's story about cooking French fries with horse fat she considered secretly ordering some from glue factories in Belgium. Ridiculous. But why not suet? Didn't McDonald's use beef fat to make French fries before switching to vegetable oil? Some say they were never the same after.

Few people were afraid of eating beef anymore. The BSE scare never hit the US, and now that the low-carb craze was spreading people were actually anxious to eat beef in any form. Maybe even lard would do. She could picture Emeril Lagasse crunching away in an ad, rolling his eyes, "OH... it's a pork fat thing." But then, he'd want his name on the product.

How she finally settled upon the perfect frying medium was a matter as fortuitous as it was a recourse of desperation. You see, she had spent a fortune on equipment. A month had passed without a product line, without a single contract, without a penny of profit. There weren't even samples to send to potential customers. Just dozens of bags of "research and development." Both Suri and Ruth had begun to tire of tasting tests. They needed a minor miracle at this point. Not that he pressured her. But she began to grow desperate, wildly so, to create the perfect chip. It was an obsession that drove her to distraction. And she was not about to let Suri down. He was her silent investor at this point, but her secret passion as well. She was creating these chips for him, and until she pleased him, she could not rest. She would not go to him for more money either. The $30,000 start up had all been spent. Rent on the factory would be due in a few days, plus the utility bills, expenses in ingredients and all the rest. She needed to act now, quickly and decisively. It was in this state of mind that she made this fateful move.

One afternoon she went to visit Suri, entering through the back porch of the office so as not to disturb the patients—who were at this point thick in the waiting room. There on the porch as always were the gleaming yellow canisters with the yellow biohazard sign across the side. Without thinking she grabbed one, threw it in the back seat of her car and drove back to the factory. Of course she would have to replace it. Why not just put it back, maybe the pick up man hadn't even come yet. What a stupid thing to do. Of course it will be noticed. You can't just walk off with 20 pounds of fat. Can you? Just to play it safe, she emptied the fat into a plastic bucket, labeled it "suette" and filled the canister back up with beef fat. It was actually the last frying medium she had left. Apart from the liposuction fat, there was nothing left. Not a drop.

The next day, she took the refilled canister and replaced it among those piled up that day. Even still 20 pounds wouldn't go very far. She had to repeat the heist. Soon she knew exactly when the nurses placed the canisters outside and when the pick man came to get them. What she would do next was not clear. But she felt she had to at least give it a shot. This was her very last chance before bankruptcy and without any doubt losing the man she now knew she too was growing to love.

The thick yellow fat was glistening in the white plastic bucket. Far more solid than it would have been in a thigh or buttock. Apart from a little anesthetic injected during the operation, the fat was completely uncontaminated. And just as in the human body, the drugs wore off after a few hours. So it should be fine for cooking. She loaded it into the fryer. A full 80 pounds. Enough to fill a small woman. It turned out the fat had a very high smoking point, a pleasant nutty aroma when heated that would surely compliment that exotic ingredients beautifully. Almost like argan oil in its rich unctuousness. The chips came out lightly brown, very crisp and looking utterly perfect.

At first she thought she could never actually taste one. She could put them in packages, list it as suet in the ingredients and people would never know anything. But how could she promote a product she had never actually tasted? So reluctantly, she brought the chip to her lips. It was dusted with shiitake and miso powder. It smelled absolutely divine. And the taste, was just miraculous. Crisp, heavenly, light, with flavors that just resonated in the mouth. And so the name was born. Miracle chips.

―

With new-found confidence, a product that she was sure could sweep the marketplace, she suddenly became radiant, no, irresistible. More charming than Suri had ever known her to be. The business was on its way. She also quietly surrendered to his advances.

She was at his house one evening. They rarely met at this time. She usually spent the evening snacking while he worked late. But tonight he invited her over. She brought the latest flavor for him to taste—nuoc mam, chili, lime. It was strong enough that a man with more than a passing familiarity with the smell of human fat would not raise an eyebrow. By this point she had no qualms about eating them. And he had tasted a few. But this time she intended to eat the whole bag with him. She also promised him eventually she'd make a garam masala and yoghurt chip.

He bit in, and with no exaggeration, they were a revelation. The experience was absolutely ecstatic. It was as if he had tasted real food for the very first time. Heavenly food. His eyes rolled back into his head with the first cataclysmic crunch. They enjoyed a few together, beginning to breath more heavily. Was it the heat of the chilies or the strange erotic pleasure they were now getting from the lowly act of snacking? Something about the chips was miraculous. Their eyes met as they never had before, and they looked deeply at each other, so close together that their eyes crossed, everything went blurry, and then Suri imagined that he could see a third eye on Ruth's forehead. An optical illusion, of course. They kissed passionately, grasped each others' bodies and somehow found themselves materially transported to the bedroom where they engaged in the most passionate love-making either had ever experienced.

—

So Suri's plan had worked perfectly, as had Ruth's. In a way. The chips were selling like mad. Foodies and critics alike hailed miracle chips as the greatest thing to hit the market that decade. Junk food for gourmets. A decadent chip to satisfy the most discriminating palate. Sales went through the roof. Geoffrey Gage was seen with a bag of Miracle Chips on Rodeo Drive. During an interview he was actually munching them blithely while answering questions. He was wittier than ever, sophisticated, the common man's actor with panache and style. It was probably just enthusiasm for the opening of his new film, but viewers could not help but be seduced by his charm as he groped in the bag for the last few greasy chips. The clip even made its way to CNN. A week later the film broke box office records.

Ruth of course noticed the commotion, the photo opportunities, and even considered hiring him as an official spokesman. If he could be seen on TV with greasy fingers munching chips, who was next? Reginald Frump?

Miracles began to proliferate in such dizzying succession that no one could keep track. The skeptical among observers were quick to point out that these events were the natural culmination of long hard years of research, or that unrecognized talent had accidentally been thrown into relief. Few could deny that such a spate of inexplicable phenomena was a rare historical occurrence. Among the early Christian martyrs, of course, then again in the Middle Ages, the world was filled with levitating nuns and monks performing miraculous feats of fasting—but in the 21st century? Healing the sick too? People getting up and leaving their hospital beds after long debilitating illnesses such as TB, cancer and Parkinson's disease?

There were other miracles too—inventions that made people's heads spin with wonder—a solar powered car, a machine for desalinating seawater at a low cost, so that the water supply would never be a problem again. Then came the promise of a new safe energy source that would end the world's dependence on fossil fuels.

How could anyone have anticipated that after years of fruitless negotiations over issues of sovereignty in several Middle Eastern states, the occupying troops and rebel forces would merely lay their weapons down on their own volition and walk away peacefully? Something had to link these unrelated events. There was only one person in a position to answer the question, and she was not about to suggest that talent, creativity and even miracles came at a strange grisly price.

Still, how long could she keep this up without Suri finding out? What would he think when he did? He couldn't deny all the wonderful things happening.

The troops disobeying orders and dropping their guns was the first miracle Ruth believed she could trace back to the chips. It was merely one week before that she had filled an order to the armed forces for an ample supply to the soldiers who had grown bored with the typical barbecue or sour cream flavors. A black market in designer chips had already surfaced and the military merely thought that if they controlled the supply it would be much safer. Maybe it was just wishful thinking, but Ruth believed the peace had something to do with the chips.

The strange cures were a little more difficult to take credit for. But it was nonetheless true that researchers had recently found that in those patients with an unusually high level of response to conventional medicines, each had an elevated level of a certain lipid, somewhat different than that normally found in the human body. It was chemically similar, but slightly altered.

The scientists were never able to trace this lipid factor back to the chips that each of these patients had tried at least once, many of whom had become addicts. But it was clear to Suri and Ruth that their chips must have played a role. Their suspicions were confirmed when researchers were able to replicate the mutated lipid and they claimed that it resembled nothing more than a fat that has begun to degrade slightly, as after heating, when frying foods. But somehow it became lodged in the body where it has a positive effect on the targeting and rate of absorption of standard medicines. They had quickly applied to the FDA to use the lipid molecule for a wide range of therapies.

Then there were more prosaic accomplishments: brilliant new novels, new experimental techniques in the arts and cinema, a run of records broken in athletic events. No one could have imagined that all these people ate miracle chips. Ruth however recognized that whatever the cost, the infinite good accruing in the world more than made up for the fact that she was turning people into cannibals without their knowing it. With this logic, she began to step up production. The facilities were expanded; more fryers were added. She even suggested to Suri that he negotiate with fellow cosmetic surgeons throughout the county to pool their resources in biomedical waste disposal, and found his own company to pick and "dispose" of fat at dramatically cut rates.

Ruth began to fill the fryers slightly too high, hiring a few workers who would run the plant through a night shift—but who would never see the canisters that arrived mid-day. All this in the name of benevolence. New flavors were tested and approved. The Ghanian yam chips with peanut sauce were a whole new direction for the company, and the public was dumbfounded by their richness and depth of flavor. Was it palm oil? The African spices?

Still, no one made a connection between miracle chips and miracles. Except for one man, whom few people apart from insomniacs had ever heard of. It was the late night fat guru, Athram Travets. In one of his typical fulminations, he began to suggest that the miracles were not coincidental. They were all connected to fat. Just as were the miracles of Jesus and his disciples, Catherine of Siena, St. Louis the Pious. They were all anointed and consumed fat. Their very pores exuded unction. This is why saints emit a sweet fragrance for years after death. This is why miracles continue to happen in the presence of their bones. God Himself dreamed of savoring the smoke of the perfect sacrifice, Abraham's son Isaac, and so should people whose fat was created in his own image. All the saints had tasted the celestial ambrosia, had fed on fat, just as God, bodiless, was nourished with smoke from the whole offerings.

None of this made much sense. And Ruth was certain that she had never said miracle and chips in the same sentence. But somehow every word from his mouth seemed to accuse her. She panicked and tried to phone the station. Of course this was a pre-recorded infomercial. The cable station had no idea when or where this was recorded. She phoned Suri next, in a state of desperation, but unable to explain why. He assured her it was just stress, too much work, expansion too quickly. But she knew it was some species of guilt. Though no one was ever hurt, and so much good was being done, there was something painfully wrong. And she knew someone would find out eventually, probably Suri first. He tried to calm her as best he could, and they spoke for a good 45 minutes.

Their conversation went on too long. All the while the police were trying to reach them. One of the new workers had accidentally tipped over a full and bubbling fryer. She wasn't hurt, but the fire had now engulfed the entire factory. In the half hour it took them to get to the site, the conflagration had spread and three fire trucks were hosing it down at full force, but to little avail.

The smoke ascended from the top half of the building, now resembling a kind of altar with the lower cinder blocks still in place and flames dripping from the roof-line.

And then a strange intoxicating aroma suffused throughout the city. Not of chili or lime or truffle infusions, but something enchanting and sweet. It wafted under doors and through cracks in the windowpanes. It seeped up through floorboards and up from elevator shafts. That night the city slept soundly, as if sated for the first time in its life. Anxieties melted away, desires were blissfully fulfilled, in this ethereal green smoke of dreams.

In the morning it was all over. Miracles came to a sudden halt. Human lives were again fraught with pain and misery. The souls of the damned returned to their accustomed torments. Soldiers fought, the sick suffered, grandiose plans crumbled to pieces. All that remained of the factory the next day was a pile of scorched rubble. Among the ashes there was one small greenish lump of fat, which a threadbare cat cautiously sniffed and ate.

DELICACY

John Axel Kohagen

The décor set entirely the wrong mood for our dinner, but that was to be expected. Don Sharvel was a genius in regards to his cooking, not in regards to his sense of style. His style reflected the immensity of ego in his heart, and it was an indicator of the man's personal reserve of bombast. Black velvet throws adorned a bevy of dark wooden antique furniture. Candles illuminated tapestries that I fathomed were probably quite expensive. The whole room was under lit to the point of being murky, making it seem cavernous rather than elitist, cluttered rather than composed.

But I wasn't joining Don for the ambience.

"I'm glad you came," Don said. He motioned for me to sit down, and then he sat himself. Don was a squat man, not very tall but with such a leonine demeanor that he looked regal in his chair, even though I noticed his feet had to strain to touch the ground. "You'll be able to taste first," he continued, and here he giggled. His giggle indicated a crack in the majesty, more jester than ruler.

"Maybe I just didn't have a whole lot of other things to do," I said. I sat down, my ancient chair creaking less than his. Time has whittled me down into a thin stalk, and left my eyes sunken into my head to finish the tale. Don is a sated man; I am still hungry for substance in my life.

"The salad," Don announced, as our server brought us out the first course. The greens on my plate carried a message to me, as I know Don would never serve me a meal he had not personally planned every bite of. The dressing was quite traditional, and the lettuce appeared to have been of the finest quality. The real message was conveyed by combining this lettuce with greenery more reflective of current taste trends favoring health food and more variety in salad. A mixture of old and new, showing a dish perfectly in harmony with its past and its future. I believe I was to infer the same thing about Don.

"Your restaurant failed," he said. He said it like he had thought it so many times that saying it slow was hard. His brow furrowed and his head leaned down as he said it, making his effort obvious. "You understand why?"

"I know what you'll say," I said. The meal would've gone better with wine, but my host has only provided me with sparkling water.

"But you came," he said. He nodded a little as he said this, and now I could tell he was posturing. That was the one thing all of the chefs never understood about him. He wore his self-importance unevenly; it was a lying garment that happened to match his demeanor. If you understood that, you could tolerate him. Most of our chefs couldn't stand him, even though they couldn't deny his skill. "You came because you knew I had something you wanted, and you knew you'd take it."

"Well, we'll see if it's worth the trip, first, before we start kissing each others' asses," I said.

"Very well," he said. He did not posture, and I noted this as odd, but I continued to eat.

Really, he and I never had much to say to each other. The food that lay between was, as always, the only link that connected us as human beings. He was a passionate egoist; I was simply trying to get by in a competitive world. He had convictions and I had calculations.

We met in culinary school because I decided to let him break the air for me, so I could calmly ride in his wake. He strutted about as if he would one day own the place, and I made sure he noticed I was always behind him, as if I would witness the bill of sale.

I did this because, unlike him, I was never very good at being a chef. Maybe that isn't quite accurate. I was always good at being a chef, but I was never anything other than proficient. There was nothing in my knife cuts, my recipe choices, or my plating that could not have been done by some sort of soulless automaton.

The next course came out—a shrimp cocktail arranged just so.

"Pretty tame," I told him. I was no longer the nervous child hiding in his shadow. Time and tide had turned me into a bitter smear of a man.

"It's an appetizer," he said. "I felt obliged. The main course is the meaning of our visit."

He had asked me to come help him reclaim what was rightfully his. Considering his ego, I could only assume that meant control of the world. The look in his eyes, the shark of his smile, the very angle of his madman's lean back into his chair did not discredit this assumption.

His downfall came late in his career, after he and I had graduated. He had enough money for him to be able to go on a string of unpaid apprenticeships, apprenticing himself to the masters with the sole goal of becoming the best chef in the world. In 1983 he had applied to take the test to become a Certified Master Chef with the American Culinary Foundation. Becoming a CMC is a difficult task, so difficult that there were only seventy American chefs to achieve the honor in about a quarter century of its having been created. He most certainly would have made it, but days before his testing was schedule he abandoned the test. He was apparently half naked and spouting gibberish, complaining that it was all the same food, that there was no point. This is what I heard, at least.

"You made it sound like whatever it was you had to show me would bring my restaurant back," I said. I wanted the restaurant back, and badly. It had succeeded. My lifetime of playing it safe, of following trends and leaving them when they became unprofitable, turned into a respectable upscale restaurant in Minneapolis, Minnesota. It wasn't Rome, or New York, but it was somewhere and I had made a mark there.

He laughed then.

"God himself could not bring your restaurant back," he replied, full of barbarism. "You should know that. You're the one who pissed it away."

It was true. The plan had been ingenious in the beginning. I simply hired sous chefs who were more up on the trends than I, advertised their skills until it was no longer useful to do so, and then fired them and replaced them with the next culinary sensation I could find. There was always someone else. As executive chef, I handled the books and stayed in my own little office. I kept the right people happy and glad-handed my way through as many customers as I had to. Being obsequious appears to be one of my few natural gifts.

"And that's why there's no wine at the table," I said. "Because of my drinking."

"No, it wasn't the wine," he replied. "The drinking started because you had nothing better to do. And why was that? Because you were bored with the food. It had lost its life."

"Did you really say something like that when you stumbled away from the CMC test?" I asked. "I heard you were one step away from being certifiable."

Somehow, he liked this. It made his sloppy, food-flecked mouth grin.

"Yes. Yes, I did. And I meant it. It's all the same, and it has been for years and years. Years and years of people like us, cooking the same things. It's all just food. If we don't do something about that, it becomes the same thing going in as it is going out, doesn't it?"

At this moment the main course arrived.

It came to my part of the table with pomp and circumstance usually reserved for important rituals of religion, but what it was did not live up to the expectations. It was a pork loin, garnished in a sauce that looked very Bavarian. There were odd little mushrooms scattered about, in that artfully planned scattershot that chefs learn. A small half loaf of bread, on its own plate, completed the meal.

His meal came with wine at this point. He tasted his wine and then stood and toasted me.

"William Shakespeare, in Hamlet, once wrote that 'a king may go a progress through the guts of a beggar.' It is my humble opinion that that beggar is the true king." And here he sipped. I eyed him cruelly. "Well, I do know you have a problem with the stuff, and I do need you sober. I don't see why that should stop me from imbibing."

I did have a problem, and I had been sober for over a year now, though the night was beginning to wear on me.

It had been the drinking, in all honesty, that had done my little restaurant in. The drinking and a bastard named Dean Ian. Dean Ian had a reputation as a hot chef to watch, so I snatched him up and used him to replace my most recent hire. But Dean was too clever to play along. He heard war stories from the line cooks, so he started noticing things. Like how much alcohol never made it to the bar but went straight to my office. Or perhaps he noticed certain employees were in that office for far too long, and that there were looks exchanged. I do not know what exactly he noted, but he did a good enough job of it that my backers, who owned over fifty percent of the restaurant together, forced me out for a very modest amount of money. Dean took over, made some changes, and my whole cautious empire toppled under his young and foolhardy hand. This somehow sullied me, and now my attempts to start a new restaurant have met with shut doors.

If the man across from me had a way to save my restaurant that didn't involve any kind of satanic pact, I would be willing to listen. But the pork loin before me did not look like an answer.

"I can get this at the Sizzler," I said. I poured another Perrier, pretending like it had more to it than just water.

"Taste," he said. His smile was cherubic; the drool was not.

I did so, and then I actually did believe him. The pork loin had a flavor I hadn't tasted before. Subtle, but unmistakable. The mushrooms added the same gentle bite. Even the bread was more than just bread. There was an addition to this meal that made the banal somehow sublime. I felt as if I was crossing over a threshold just by eating.

"Okay, so what's the catch?" I asked. I tried the bread next. It had a very earthy taste to it, almost old world. It was immaculately done, but somehow seemed less cutting edge than I had expected. Still, there was something in the taste that eluded me.

"There are no surprises," he said. "The same principles of cooking are applied here. Well-fed animals. The proper microbes necessary to raise the bread. Mushrooms picked from the right environment."

I raised an eyebrow but, hooked, I continued eating. The mushrooms were totally new, totally different. Maybe that's what this was all about. He was showing me off a new mushroom. This was different, of course, but it didn't seem to match up with his bravado.

"Much of this involves the death of an organism, in a way. Animals are fed from other animals. Mushrooms eat off of decay. There is even consumption in the act of bread rising, because the yeast must be fed. There must be a death to feed the living. An organism must die."

"And?" I asked. Slightly impatient.

"A human is an organism, correct?" He let it sink in. My food did not look the same, though I did not regret eating it. I was not nudged by a pang of nausea. I was simply beside myself.

"Could be the organism the mushrooms you are eating grew from. Could have provided the microbes necessary to raise that bread, though slightly modified from traditional yeast. Could even have fed the pig you are now feeding from. Are you tasting the journey Shakespeare wrote of?"

"It's illegal," I said. Laughing the man off.

"Not terribly. I am not a killer. I tried to procure the best ingredients I could, but there are not many available. Medical schools shoot them full of nasty chemicals, as do mortuaries. I have to wait for clean John Does and Jane Does, and then place the right bribes. Perhaps the success of your new restaurant will change that, will make the procuring of the right ingredients routine."

"My new restaurant?"

"I will back you, and I will supply the menu. You will handle the customers. Make them feel appreciated. Like you're good at it. I need that now. Arrogance sells few dinners."

"Why?" I said. "If people knew what we were serving them."

"We'll tell them," he said. He giggled and he wiggled his eyebrows. "We'll tell them exactly what they're eating and we'll bribe the right people and they'll be lining up to make a reservation."

"Why?" I asked.

"Because no one has ever been happy with their meal. At any restaurant, at any time. Not really. They always expected something more when they ordered, a magical property that no food can seem to have. I searched for it from chef to chef, and it frustrated me until I dropped out of CMC testing.

"People like to taste death, just a little. It's why they go out. They want to taste something they can't have in their homes, something impossible. Something they've never seen before, right? Every menu has always promised a taste of that which is forbidden, which cannot be explained. The sublime. Ridiculous chain restaurants use it to sell fattening brownie desserts. Better restaurants hint at it with subtlety, by giving menus that look like hymnals and nonsense like that. Our restaurant will actually use it as a seasoning, and people's bellies will finally be properly full. Just as yours is now, correct?"

It was.

"It's not even morbid, really. It's just a remembering you're part of the circle of things, isn't it?"

"I'll do it," I said. In truth, I did find it morbid and disturbed, though God help me, I understood what he said. I wasn't proud of my decision. But it would get me my restaurant again, my chance to please others. It would fill my belly in another way.

"I knew you would," he said. "But, if you hadn't just yet, there is always dessert."

The Watchman's Secret

Harry Brown

"In the year 1820 the ship Essex, Captain Pollard, of Nantucket, was cruising in the Pacific Ocean. One day she saw spouts, lowered her boats, and gave chase to a shoal of sperm whales. Ere long, several of the whales were wounded; when, suddenly, a very large whale escaping from the boats, issued from the shoal and bore directly down upon the ship. Dashing his forehead against her hull, he so stove her in, that... she settled down and fell over.... After the severest exposure, part of the crew reached the land in their boats." Herman Melville, *Moby-Dick*

Nantucket Quay, 1866

Not long ago, one might have heard the hammers beating molten iron into the elegant, evil shape of the harpoon; or the pilot's bell guiding traffic in the harbor; or the rousing cries of the dockworkers welcoming home a whale ship low in the water and laden with oil. Now, the ships are lashed to the pilings, and one hears only the groan of their aging timbers and the lapping of the tide against their hulls.

It has stunned the islanders to see the fishery ruined so quickly. Confederate raiders decimated the Yankee whaling fleet during the war, and the shipwrights have not rushed to rebuild. Reservoirs of petroleum, discovered in Pennsylvania less than a decade ago, have already begun to replace whale oil as the nation's source of light. The few ships that remain venture farther now, and for lesser rewards, sailing to glacial seas only to find the shoals vanished, hunted nearly to extinction. Soon, tourists rather than whales will provide Nantucket with its trade.

But aspiration dies harder than opportunity, and still the boys here dream of becoming whale men like their fathers. On warm evenings, we might imagine, one of them lingers on the wharf. An unfortunate heir, he has one of the great old names of the island—Coffin or Folger or Macy. His father, first mate aboard the whale ship *Providence* or some other propitiously named vessel, drowned at some empty meridian east of New

Zealand. The boy hardly knew him—his time at home was so rare—but he keeps by his bed a gift his father once gave to his mother: a piece of scrimshaw incised with a three-masted whaler, an American eagle, and a banner unfurled in its talons—"LIBERTY." The boy is destined for the textile factory in New Bedford.

We might imagine, though, while he is still a boy, he goes to meet an old watchman who sometimes tells him of his voyages as a whale master. The old man calls the boy "Mister," as he would call a mate, and smiles often. But his stories are strange and filled with horror: an entire island consumed by flame, a ship stove by a monstrous whale, and men transformed by hunger into living corpses—and worse. The boy's mother tells him that the old man is cursed; others say he is a murderer. Most of the islanders, nonetheless, call him Captain. Who could search themselves, after all, and know that he could endure what Pollard endured?

The Captain's Lot

At twenty-eight, George Pollard had the trust of the best men in Nantucket. In June 1819, he took the deacon's daughter for his wife, and in August he took command of the *Essex*, a whale ship famed for good fortune. Ignoring the summer's ill omens—the shooting stars and the grasshoppers in the turnip fields—he bid farewell to his young wife and, with his crew of twenty-one, made for the Offshore Ground west of Chile.

Pollard fairly disliked his first mate, Owen Chase, whom he long knew as a brazen lad. Yet, for all his cheek, Chase was a worthy whale hunter, quick to the kill, and a help among so many green hands. Most of them were just boys, or landsmen, or runaway slaves. They faltered, and they complained, and once Pollard had to threaten them with flogging. One absconded in Peru, and in the Galapagos another was careless with his tinderbox. The fire burned for days, leaving Charles Island black and lifeless. The crew laughed at the mischief, but Pollard looked on the desolation more ruefully. For many years, sailors would find no provision there.

They took three hundred of the great tortoises from the Galapagos, casting them like stones into the hold until they could fit no more. Their soft, savory flesh would sustain the crew for many months, and—Pollard had been told—the creatures could live almost indefinitely without food or water. He ordered the crew to take no pains to feed the tortoises, as they did with the pigs, though he observed the animals creep along the deck in slow desperation, chewing wood and hemp and leather.

Years later, the writers, the mariners, the curious visitors, would ask Pollard about the attack of November 20, 1821. No one had ever known such a thing: a whale, as if sentient, to turn on a ship and sink it. Pollard would inevitably disappoint them, telling them honestly that he had not seen the monster. He was in his whaleboat, chivvying the shoal, when he noticed the masts fall below the horizon. When Pollard and second mate Matthew Joy returned to the place where the ship had been, they found Chase and the others huddled fearfully in their boat. "My God," Pollard asked his first mate, "where is the ship?"

Chase's boat had been damaged in pursuit of the shoal. He had returned to the ship to make repairs when a bull, fully as large as the *Essex* herself, charged the bow and crushed the hull. She lay capsized there, while the pigs and tortoises paddled and dipped among the flotsam, drowning. They salvaged provisions from the wreckage, gathering in each of the three boats two hundred pounds of hardtack, two tortoises, and a cask of fresh water. Two of the boats rescued a pig. They found sextants and pistols and, rigging each boat with gunwales and sails, they reckoned a long voyage in open boats.

Pollard believed they could reach the Marquesas, some six hundred leagues southwest, but Chase convinced the crew that cannibals lurked there and proposed a much longer, much more difficult voyage to the South American coast, nearly a thousand leagues distant. There had been missionaries and safe harbors in French Polynesia since the turn of the century, but the crew, who knew little of navigation or the Marquesas, feared the imagined cannibals more than starvation and favored Chase's plan. They sailed east, against the current. Their rations, Pollard knew, would not last.

Two months in open boats brought them to the limit of their endurance. Sun and salt spray parched their skin; their tongues swelled and left them unable to speak; and dreams of banquets plagued their sleep before they awoke in bilge water, weeping. They consumed their tortoises, their hardtack and water, and then they chewed strips of leather and drank their urine. Matthew Joy died first, and five others followed him. The rest survived on the flesh of their dead mates for three more weeks. Squalls separated the boats and, too weak to navigate, they were lost.

In Pollard's boat, hope faded. He later recalled, "We looked at each other with horrid thoughts in our mind. I am sure we loved one another as brothers all the time; and yet our looks told plainly what must be done." There were three boys with Pollard: Owen Coffin, Charles Ramsdell, and Barzillai Ray. They were Nantucketers all, fatherless all, the sons of lost whalers, and friends since boyhood. Pollard himself was cousin to Coffin. Before the *Essex* departed, the captain promised his aunt, Nancy Coffin, that he would preserve her son and bring him home safely. Now, the four drew lots to see who would die to feed the others.

This game at the dark heart of the *Essex* story has remained inscrutable to history, a peculiar intimacy speculated by observers but kept secret by the survivors. We have only secondhand accounts of what happened in Pollard's boat on February 6, 1821, testimony from those who were in Chase's boat or those who spoke to Pollard or Ramsdell later. Beyond that, we have only vaguely informed conjecture or rumor.

In the public letter that first reported the wreck to Nantucket, Aaron Paddack, captain of one of the vessels that taxied the survivors to safety, writes simply, "the captain and the three others that remained with him were reduced to the deplorable necessity of casting lots to see who should be sacrificed to prolong the existence of the others. The lot fell to Owen Coffin, who with composure and resignation submitted to his fate." Chase, who published the most widely read narrative of the *Essex* disaster in November 1821, follows Paddack's report, explaining that Coffin drew the fatal chance and "with great fortitude and resignation submitted to his fate." Chase further relates that Pollard, Ramsdell, and Ray drew lots again to decide who would execute Coffin, and that Ramsdell "had the hard fortune." Thomas Nickerson, the *Essex* cabin boy, had been with Chase, and in his memoirs he repeats Chase's story. Coffin, he writes, drew his lot and "with great fortitude and resignation cheerfully smiled at his fate at this awful moment." Pollard offered to take his cousin's place, Nickerson recalls, but Coffin refused and "placed himself in firm position to receive his death." Ramsdell, Nickerson agrees, was executioner.

But Chase and Nickerson had drifted more than a hundred miles from Pollard's boat by that time and in fact witnessed nothing. Historians agree that Chase composed his *Narrative of the Wreck of the Whale Ship* Essex to redeem his reputation and advertise his worth as a potential whale master. Nathaniel Philbrick, whose book, *In the Heart of the Sea*, has lately renewed interest in the *Essex* story, suggests, "...by keeping many of the most disturbing and problematic aspects of the disaster offstage, Chase transforms the story of the *Essex* into a personal tale of trial and triumph." The story, as Chase told it, cast both Pollard and Coffin as heroes and surely pleased readers, who could find in the mariners' suffering something more ideal than the morbid lesson of men laid low by hunger.

In private correspondence, however, Nickerson contradicts his own memoir. He has the story, he says, from Ramsdell, who names Pollard as executioner. The captain, Ramsdell told Nickerson, drew the second lot and shot his cousin. "For a long time," Nickerson writes, Pollard "declared that he would never do it, but finally had to submit." Historians mainly dismiss Nickerson's letter as error, since it does not agree with most other accounts, but testimony from those who heard from Pollard himself likewise casts some doubt on the accepted story of "fortitude and resignation." American Navy lieutenant Charles Wilkes, who would later lead the United

States' first expedition to the Antarctic, met Pollard in 1822. In his memoirs, he recalls simply that the drawing of lots provoked "intense suffering" and concludes, "I cannot state the narrative of this; it is too horrible to be related as it was told to me." In April 1823, the English missionaries Daniel Tyerman and George Bennet also met Pollard, whose own words they record in their journal. When Coffin drew his lot, Pollard said, "My lad, my lad, if you don't like your lot, I'll shoot the first man that touches you." Coffin replied, "I like it as well as any other." But Pollard does not tell the missionaries who executed Coffin. "My head," he told them, "is on fire with the recollection."

Considering these obscurities, we suspect that the full story of Owen Coffin's death has not been told. Save for a few strained confidences, Pollard and Ramsdell themselves—the only two survivors of that boat—have left us no clue. In Nantucket, uncertainty gave way to rumor. Was it Pollard who shot Coffin, his own kin? Or was it Pollard himself who drew the fatal lot? Joseph Phinney, an islander who knew Pollard, writes, "The story goes, they drew lots as to who would die for the others, and the man who drew the lot had his place taken by a young boy who insisted on dying instead of the older man. ...Well, I don't know how true it is. Anyway, there was some mystery."

On February 18 the whaler *India* rescued Chase, Nickerson, and Benjamin Lawrence. The three had survived in their boat on the flesh of Isaac Cole, who had died on February 8. On February 23, the whaler *Dauphin* rescued Pollard and Ramsdell. They were lying in the bilge, sucking the bones of Barzillai Ray, who had expired on February 11. The third boat was never found.

When Pollard came home on August 5, 1821, almost two thousand Nantucketers greeted him on the quay. The crowd parted as he walked to the home of his aunt, Nancy Coffin, to convey his sorrow. She could not forgive him.

The islanders embraced Pollard nonetheless, and he was given another command, the *Two Brothers*. When that ship wrecked on an uncharted reef west of Hawaii in February 1823, though, Pollard's career as a whale master ended. No one would trust him a third time. He became a night watchman and, until his death in 1870, lived on Centre Street with his wife—peacefully though perhaps not quite happily. All his life he had believed that the only right work for a man was aboard a whale ship. On his rounds he carried a long hickory pole with a rough iron hook at the end—he called it his harpoon. He used it to reach the street lamps and, sometimes, to menace a child playfully, but even when there were no street lamps or children to tend, he held it firm.

A Visit on Centre Street

On July 6, 1852, Herman Melville and his father-in-law, Judge Lemuel Shaw, boarded the ferry from New Bedford to Nantucket, where the judge had business. They arrived toward evening and took rooms at the Ocean House on Centre Street. The next day, with Judge Shaw's affairs concluded, the two dined with the astronomer William Mitchell and his daughter Maria, who enchanted Herman with her telescope and her naming of the stars. In such wonderful company, the judge could not comprehend his son in law's morbid curiosity about George Pollard. Yet Melville spoke of the man since they boarded the ferry and seemed pleased when they found a boardinghouse so near Pollard's residence. The judge, a stern landsman, did not brook the custom of the sea, as men sometimes called the game that Pollard and Ramsdell played in 1821. Had they come to Shaw's court, he might have found them guilty of murder. Still, Melville had just finished *Moby-Dick* a year ago and insisted on visiting Pollard the next day.

Neither Melville, nor Shaw, nor Pollard left a detailed record of that visit on July 8, 1852. In his correspondence, Shaw simply remembers Pollard as one of several persons he and Melville visited that day. Melville does not speak of the visit itself, only his impression of Pollard: "To the islanders he was a nobody—to me, the most impressive man, though wholly unassuming, even humble—that I ever encountered." What was it in Pollard's speech or manner that impressed Melville so profoundly? What words might the young writer and the aging watchman have shared that day?

We may assume that they exchanged a cordial Yankee greeting: stiff, plain, and frank. Yet Pollard might have regarded Melville with some suspicion, as a novelist, perhaps, who traded on his meager, inglorious experiences at sea. Melville had famously absconded from a whale ship, broken his contract. He complained of mistreatment by his captain, as Pollard's crews had sometimes complained, but more likely, he preferred the degenerate luxuries of Nuku Hiva than the honest work of a whale hunter. Or Pollard might have thought more charitably of the young writer. Melville, after all, proved gracious. He did not he ask about Owen Coffin, as other writers did. Perhaps the two spoke of the enchantment of the Galapagos or discussed the late successes of Charles Wilkes, who had taken his federal ships to edge of the known world. Nantucket whalers, Pollard swore, broke ice at those latitudes long before Wilkes went there.

An extract from *Moby-Dick* had appeared in the Nantucket *Inquirer* the previous November. Pollard had been too sleepy to read it then, heavy as it was with philosophy, but perhaps he offered Melville an awkward compliment, or a joke: he always enjoyed nautical stories, but he found the idea of a whale attacking a ship wholly fantastical! Melville, Pollard, even Shaw, would have laughed warmly, and then the judge, the most skilled gentleman among them, would have risen from his seat and offered his regrets. He and Melville were traveling to Martha's Vineyard in the morning and had to bid farewell to Professor Mitchell and his daughter before dinner. Pollard, probably, was relieved to see the judge go—such significant men rarely called on him since he had become a watchman. The young writer, though, seemed a good chap. He did not trim his beard so neat, nor wear his coat so prim as they did in Boston. He was not a whale man, surely, but he might have passed for an islander.

In his first novel, *Typee*, Melville describes his adventures in the Pacific with puerile audacity, decrying the brutality of colonials and mocking the righteousness of missionaries, but taking great pleasure in swimming nude with the island girls and exposing the cannibalism of the native Polynesians as a lurid spectacle. In *Moby-Dick*, he speaks of cannibalism more abstractly, as a metaphor for civilized depravities. He had not confronted the difficult problem of white men pressed to atrocity by something as simple and inevitable as hunger. After meeting Pollard, though, Melville's perspective seemed to change. He had been an architect of sensation and symbol. Now, he was more fascinated by character; not trauma but its silent, interior aftermath, and the stalwart, lonely people who bear the burden of memory.

In August 1852, a month after he returned from his tour of the islands with Judge Shaw, Melville wrote to his friend, Nathaniel Hawthorne, expressing his sympathy for the women in Nantucket who with great patience endure the long absences of their husbands. He proposed an idea to Hawthorne: a story of a mariner's widow—Agatha, he calls her—who waits and watches for her husband, gone to sea and long overdue. He sketches the setting of Agatha's story—a stark island of cliffs and high pastures off the coast of Maine—and describes the essence of the tragedy. Agatha's husband does not come home; he has married another woman far away. And yet she waits for the mail and bolsters the stonewalls against the encroaching waves and receives counsel from her father, the lone lighthouse keeper. Melville explains to Hawthorne, "The father of Agatha must be an old widower—a man of the sea, but early driven away from it by repeated disasters. Hence, is he subdued and quiet and wise in his life. And now he tends a lighthouse, to warn people from those very perils, from which he himself has suffered." After Hawthorne urged Melville himself to write Agatha's story, Melville labored that autumn on a new novel he called *The Isle of the Cross*. His publisher, Harper and Brothers, rejected the manuscript, and now no trace remains of this lost, literary incarnation of Captain Pollard, the humble watcher who has reconciled himself to an island purgatory.

Melville, though, did not forget Agatha's father or George Pollard, even as he left his most promising years as a writer behind him. In 1866, while Pollard paced the quay in Nantucket, regarding the still ships, Melville took a job as a customs inspector in New York, perhaps feeling the same regret and resignation he sensed in Pollard and portrayed in Agatha's father. Melville's biographers have called attention to this shared disappointment, pondering the aging Melville's eerie identification with Pollard. In *Clarel*, a narrative poem Melville finished in 1876 while still customs inspector, Pollard, though unnamed, appears again as a captain of lost ships. One wrecked on invisible rocks, the other stove by a whale, he and his men longer in their boats, starved and pressed to the "crime abhorred." Ruined, the mariner in *Clarel* becomes a lonely nocturnal sentinel:

> *A Jonah is he?—and men bruit*
> *The story. None will give him place*
> *In a third venture. Came the day*
> *Dire need constrained the man to pace*
> *A night patrolman on the quay*
> *Watching the bales till morning hour*
> *Through fair and foul. Never he smiled;*
> *Call him, and he would come; not sour*
> *In spirit, but meek and reconciled;*
> *Patient he was, he none withstood;*
> *Oft on some secret thing he would brood.*

Melville took unjust liberty, perhaps, in his portrayal. By the islanders' accounts, Pollard, though meek and reconciled, often smiled and jostled the children. But we wonder about Pollard on those long, chill nights when there was no one to humor. Melville probably shared his sense of professional disappointment, as the biographers have said, but in this final poetic rendering of Pollard, Melville places him at a distance. Although there is nothing to watch, nothing to await, he keeps vigilant. His gaze, as he turns to the sea, seems to reach to the other side of the world, and if you approached him, he may not see you, though you stood at an arm's length. But what did Melville intimate in this ancient Yankee mariner—mere cannibalism? It was well known in Nantucket, and long ago forgiven. What secret thing set him adrift?

The Watchman's Secret

If we return to the quay in 1866 and imagine again the fatherless boy there, going to meet the old watchman, we might overhear it. Not a confession, certainly—Pollard had no need. He made his peace with God if not with Nancy. One more fearful tale, rather, maybe the last one that Pollard would tell. This boy was a bit younger than Owen but very like him. Maybe his face, which indeed recalled his cousin to life, loosed Pollard's memory.

He smiled to read the accounts. He heard that Chase had his friend write the book, some fellow from Harvard College, who made them all sound like noble senators gone to their ends for the Nation of Nantucket. There was a coarse kind of heroism in that boat, probably, but they were too weak for great words, their throats utterly dry and their thoughts near deranged. Pollard protested when Charles first mentioned it. They might wait until one of them expired, not long. Barzillai said nothing, but Owen and Charles urged it. If they waited any longer, all four of them would surely die.

They had a journal there. They had given up writing weeks ago and lately tried to eat a few pages. Pollard tore four small scraps from the book, marked one of them with a smudge of ash, and placed them in a cap.

Charles drew first and collapsed with relief.

Owen drew next—the ashen lot.

He cast it overboard, as if it stung his fingers, and began to weep, too parched to shed tears, looking to Barzillai and Charles, who had run with him on the wharves when they were boys. They turned away from him now.

They did not draw lots again. Pollard was captain, and he would not ask the boys to level the pistol against Owen. Yet he felt that he could not do it himself. He took the gun from the chest and faltered, looking at the thing in his lap while Owen sobbed. He thought, for a moment, that he would shoot himself.

In an instant, it seemed, Owen stopped crying and without pause, without words, he took the pistol from Pollard's lap, held it against his temple, and fired. The body slumped on the gunwale.

He would not kill him, the watchman told the boy, but he hesitated to use the pistol on himself, and he did not close his hands when Owen reached for it. He and Charles butchered the corpse quickly enough, and relished Owen's heart before they thought to pray for his soul: Greater love hath no man… That was the lesson, he supposed, not "fortitude and resignation," which failed them all.

They agreed that Owen's mother, who married a Quaker but held fast to her Episcopalian ideas about mortal sin and suicide, should not know. When the captain of the *Dauphin* questioned them, Charles said that that he had executed Owen. Pollard supposed he felt guilty for proposing lots, for drawing life. He did not know, and they did not speak of it with each other again.

The boy, we might imagine, walked home more slowly that night, quizzical. What guilt did the watchman bear? Years later, perhaps in the factory, when he knew more about despair and the silent complicity that one person has in the fate of all others, he might think of Pollard more as Melville did. Could one kill simply by doing nothing, by watching someone else die? Was that better than firing a pistol and eating someone's heart? Pollard's story, one day, would trouble him as it troubled Melville.

For almost a quarter of a century, from the time he met him in 1852 until the time he poeticized him in 1876, Melville contemplated the captain of the *Essex*. "I have been told that Pollard the captain wrote, or caused to be wrote under his own name, his version of the story," Melville noted. "I have seen extracts purporting to be from some such work. But I have never seen the work itself." With the lost leaves of his testimony, Pollard has vanished from history like a Nantucket father gone to sea, and like the son whose wonder eclipses his memory, his eyes searching the scrimshaw again, Melville, like us, remembers him best not as a person but as a myth.

RECIPES

Hansel and Gretel Virginia Ham

Delicatessen Man: "Virginia Ham is Virginia Ham."

Irate Customer: "You call Yourself a Delicatessen Man?! Hansel and Gretel Virginia Ham tastes better! Hansel and Gretel Virginia Ham is superior! I always buy by the name Hansel and Gretel!" (*from a popular TV advertisement for "Hansel and Gretel Virginia Ham" that ran in the 1970s in the New York area*)

Dress like a witch and find a nice candy cottage to occupy somewhere deep in the woods, perhaps in Virginia, or the Black Forest. Capture your Hansel and Gretel while they nibble on the window-panes. Remove the thighs of both Hansel and Gretel, and set aside the rest for another use. Rub salt into the four thighs generously and let cure for a week. Then hang them in the chimney of your house to be gently smoked.

They will last indefinitely. Slice thinly and serve on white bread with mustard.

Ken Albala

Moque Chevre chez Maman

Milk a lactating woman, or reserve about two pints of leftover from a milk-pumping machine—only after baby has been fed, of course. The best machines are those that play "Turkey in the Straw." Heat the milk gently to about 150 degrees and add a rennet tablet. The curds should begin to separate from the whey as the temperature of the milk continues to rise. Stir gently. After holding for about 15 minutes at the lowest possible heat setting, pour the mixture into a cheesecloth-lined strainer and let the whey drain. Tie the curds up in the cheesecloth without pressing and suspend this ball from the faucet over the kitchen sink overnight. In the morning refrigerate until needed.

The flavor is reminiscent of chevre, but note that the mother's diet will significantly affect the taste and texture. Coffee and garlic come through quite powerfully. Indian food is unmistakable.

Serve on crackers to unsuspecting guests.

Ken Albala

Californian Roll

A perky young Californian girl is required for this recipe. A valley girl, if you can find one. Carefully slice thin wedges from the choicest parts (breast, thigh and buttocks), and set aside. Place a nori sheet on your bamboo roller and lay on the fresh Californian slices, some avocado, a dab of mayonnaise, and sushi rice on top of everything. Roll them inside out, with the rice on the outside, and then press the entire roll in flying fish roe to cover the outside. Slice and serve.

Ken Albala

Andes Mints

Take one good frozen soccer player and slice into very thin bite size wedges. Take a leaf of mint—or, for authenticity, a stick of double mint chewing gum—and place between two slices of soccer player. Press firmly. Wrap in green tinfoil and serve with a frozen airline dinner in a tray.

Ken Albala

Caesar Salad

First catch your emperor. He'll be easy to recognize, since he'll be the one wrapped in a bedsheet, with a wreath of bay leaves on his head, hurrying towards the forum. Assemble a group of thin friends to cut the emperor into pieces suitable for cooking, marinate in Falernian wine before grilling (but do not braise him). Slice the untimely-ripped flesh as neatly as possible, and use it to garnish a platter of Romaine lettuces that have been dressed with beaten egg, garlic and liquamen.

Gary Allen

THE MAIN COURSE

"If a man can get no other food it is more natural for him to kill another man and eat him than to starve. Our horror is rather at the circumstances that make it natural for the man to do this than at the man himself."
Samuel Butler

ANTI-MAGELLAN

Pedro Malard Monteiro

Martim Afonso de Sabrosa was ready to set sail from Brazil and go back to Portugal to sell his head to the king, when a Tupinambá Indian climbed aboard the ship, her glistening body dripping the Atlantic Ocean on the deck. I know; I saw it; I was there. You, with your big history books, I know your sort. You don't believe I watched it happen, but I tell you it's all true. I am older than houses, older than trees. Martim was the first genius I ever met. His head would have fetched a good sum of money. The naked Tupinambá had no pubic hair, and was the most beautiful living being any one had ever seen.

You have to understand, of course, that Martim Afonso wasn't going to sell his own head, and that even though the Tupinambá didn't have a single hair covering her nakedness, she was no child. The head in question had been acquired by Martim Afonso from the Dayaks, in Borneo; and the Tupinambás had no body hair at all, I swear, men and women alike.

The parrots, which we had brought to the ship to be given as presents to important people in Europe, sensed that there would be confrontation and began to cheer. No doubt in favor of the naked teenager. One of the men in the ship, Mario Glota, who could speak all the known languages in the world, would later attest that the birds were shouting "akâ," a word which means "head." The more skeptical members of the crew were exactly like you. They said that what he had heard was simply the natural noise that parrots make. There weren't so many skeptics in the world in 1531, and no man in the ship would have thought it possible for a woman to conceal a nail inside her own vagina, and hold it in place while swimming.

A decade earlier, when Magellan was in Guanabara Bay, women as beautiful and as naked as the one who stared Martim Afonso in the eye, without a touch of fear, would have sex with any man in exchange for a sharp metal object. They were primitive, they didn't have any. But by 1531, French pirates, like Pierre le Bastard, were already trading with these Indians, and giving them more axes, knives and scissors than they could possibly need. Even if that were not the case, they were furious ever since they found out about the head that Martim Afonso was carrying with him. Once, the head had been attached to Niño de Juan's neck.

Make no mistake: the Tupinambás were cannibals, all of them. Most wouldn't even bat an eyelid if Martim Afonso walked around with a dozen shrunken human heads hanging from his neck. They would merely find it curious, perhaps, but not as curious as things like mirrors or chickens. The problem was that they believed the boy was special. Niño de Juan was the son of João Lopes de Carvalho and a Tupinambá woman. He was a nine-year-old lad when his head was cut off by the Dayaks after his father abandoned him in the island of Borneo. He was last seen by his mother as he was waving goodbye, at just seven, on the deck of the Victoria, the first vessel to circumnavigate the world.

The Tupinambás knew Niño de Juan would come home to his mother. It was a prophecy. But they didn't know that he would be missing his body, and that his shriveled head would be hanging from the belt of a bearded Portuguese navigator whose notion of hygiene was disturbingly divergent from their own. The first person to spot the head and to recognize it as the head of Niño de Juan was an older Tupinambá woman who was trying to convince Martim that bathing could be fun. She was crouching down with a smiling face, splashing some of the river onto herself, when she caught a glimpse of the dry, shrunk human head dangling from Martim's waist. She thought it was some kind of animal at first, but then she squinted. Her memory quickly retrieved images of Niño de Juan waving his hand in Portuguese style. The boy looked exactly like his mother, but he had his father's nose and mannerisms. Soon enough everyone in the tribe knew about the head, and wanted it back, apparently so that they could purify it and then revive it. This is very uncharacteristic of the Tupinambás, you must understand, but the Indians we were dealing with formed a community that had recently come up with a whole new set of beliefs, many of them freshly manufactured by a Goitacá Indian who could levitate.

Some of us said it was really a miracle that the old woman recognized the head. But the more skeptical members of the crew didn't believe in miracles much. The Indians, on the other hand, thought the only effective way to teach Europeans about the joys of bathing was to get a bunch of naked Tupinambá girls to jump in the water first; that is, the conventional way.

You never saw Niño de Juan, of course, but I can tell you his nose was the most distinctive nose there ever was. So, all things considered, it's not surprising that the old woman, after seeing the round blob in the middle of a reduced head, started screaming like a parrot:

"Akâ"

The more skeptical of us also doubted that the Goitacá could levitate. We called him Tigre, because we couldn't pronounce the name by which the Tupinambás called him. The Tupinambás called him Tyrey, because they couldn't pronounce the name by which the Goitacá called himself. We don't know exactly when Tigre was captured by the Tupinambás. All we know is that he was going to be killed and eaten, but then he levitated.

The more skeptical of us found it quite decent that the Tupinambá killed their prisoners before eating them. The inquisitors in Spain thought it quite unnecessary to kill heretics before roasting them, and deemed it a heresy to eat them afterwards. I'm not sure what the Inquisition would do if they found out the crew had eaten Eduardo's left leg while starving in the Pacific. Everyone decided it was best to keep quiet about it, even though Eduardo was a Christian convert. It was only a left leg, in any case, and it did taste delicious. You have to understand, of course, that the best ingredient in any dish is a pinch of starvation.

Martim knew the Pacific Ocean was huge. He had heard it from Pigafetta, so he stocked up as much food as he could before crossing it. He took care to bring in some egg-laying chickens and wild pigs, together with all the provisions already stored in the ship. He even tied a few sea turtles to the ship. That seemed like a good idea at the time, but most of them were allegedly eaten by sharks. After the turtles, eggs, chickens, and pigs were gone, there were no sharks anywhere, no fish, and no seagulls. So the men started eating the rest of the biscuits, which were crumbling and infested with grubs. It was only after the men ate the mice, the ox hides from under the yardarms, their own belts and boots, and finally sawdust, that Niño de Juan's dried up head started looking edible. But then Eduardo offered his own leg to the crew. He offered it to everyone while he was fast asleep, and he offered it so very quietly that only Martim heard it.

"Eat my leg."

The less skeptical of us not only believed they had heard Eduardo's voice, but they also started hearing Eduardo's own leg say "Eat me," very loudly, through an aperture in the knee. The more skeptical of us could swear Eduardo's leg was very quiet while Eduardo himself was shouting, "Help." Eduardo helped himself to the biggest piece, which was only fair. The leg was so delicious that even he was in a good mood afterwards. The good mood of the crew lasted until the bone marrow was sucked dry, and before the good mood evaporated completely, Pedro Paes spotted an island on the south coast of Chile.

A bad sense of guilt only set in when the men drank fresh water on land, and gorged themselves on the food the Chonos were kind enough to provide them. Martim was the only one who hadn't lost his composure, his boots, and his head, or rather, Niño de Juan's head, which was still hanging from his belt. Martim's own head was still attached to his neck, saying things about bravery and the unfortunate accident with a cannon that had forced them to amputate Eduardo's leg.

By the time we reached Guanabara Bay, Eduardo had a sturdy wooden leg and developed a healthy habit of chewing his fingernails. He would spit out the nails, but swallow the soft bits of skin around the nails after chewing them with some relish. Sometimes he made himself bleed this way, and he'd suck his own blood when he thought no one was looking. We guessed he probably tasted better than the average human. One night, we woke up to the sound of Father Conselheiro gnawing Eduardo's wooden leg in his sleep. Since waking up a somnambulist is not advisable, we were saved the embarrassment of unclenching Father Conselheiro's jaw from around the wooden leg crafted especially by the Carijós, who are really wonderful with woodwork. Father Conselheiro didn't remember chewing on anything in his sleep, but he did complain about having fatigued jowls and peculiar dreams about the Eucharist.

Before Tigre was captured by the Tupinambá, he had tasted the flesh of all different races of men. Mario Glota, who could make out even what the Dayaks and the Maori said, had much less trouble understanding Tigre than the Tupinambás. Mario got a sea lion recipe from the Chonos, found about passing rites from the Guarani, successfully convinced the Patagonians not to eat Dieguito, and learned that Tigre started his habit of eating human liver before he could walk. The more skeptical of us thought it was unlikely that he had eaten any Mongol, but we weren't surprised to hear that, in his prime, he had covered a lot of ground and eaten not only Tubinambás, Guaranis, Carijós, but also Caiapós, Bororos, Ianomamis. He was rumored to have stolen a cannon from a Portuguese ship. He could carry and shoot the cannon from his shoulder. In this manner, he managed to kill and eat more people than any man or beast that ever lived. With this cannon, and a knack for trading with French pirates, he managed to eat Incas, Ladinos, at least three Portuguese sailors who had abandoned Cabral's expedition to run naked with the Indian women, not to mention the explorers from Germany, Holland, France, England, Italy, and Spain, which he consumed despite their heady aroma. Animals that aren't bred for consumption just don't taste as good. The Ladinos could have been kept in a controlled environment and diet, but the Spaniards made them work too hard and gave them just enough food to survive. Tigre found them a bit stringy and tough. The Incas had a decent diet, but the coca leaves kept them too alert and active. Mature men, of course, start losing their tenderness, so he was rarely tempted to eat any graying European. Young and plump Tupinambá women were the best tasting delicacies he had ever encountered, but he imagined the young fair-haired females of France would be even better, provided they were kept in a rigorous diet and were made to bathe twice a day at least a month before the slaughter. But European men seemed to prefer traveling without their women, a fact he found both unfortunate and unhealthy.

When he was captured by the Tupinambás, he was already well past his prime. He was caught by surprise, right after he had captured a Tamoio for supper. The Tupinambás took him and the Tamoio to be eaten. While the Tupinambás prepared for the feast, Tigre kept taunting his captors saying there was so much Tupinambá flesh in his entrails that they'd taste their own grandmothers when they ate him. The Tamoio went first. One of the strong men clubbed him dead with one blow to the head, which almost split the man in two and made the Tamoio's brain drop to the ground. Two women married the executioner in the following day, because it's hard to find powerful arms like that. The skinning was left to women who had already had grandchildren. The skin was not removed in a single piece, which would be more difficult to do, but in many pieces that were given the children to play with, to their absolute delight. After the man was gutted and quartered, it was Tigre's turn to go. He was standing up, as if waiting to be killed, and then suddenly he was about a foot off the ground.

After much debate, the Tupinambás decided it would be more prudent not to eat him. There were those who favored eating him because they felt that ingesting his flesh would enable them to levitate as well. There were those who thought he might be some kind of god. I rather dislike the cannibal practices of these savages, but now I know that we weren't so nice either, and admit what we did to all the Brazilian tribes wasn't so pleasant. Tigre ended up eating a share of the Tamoio. No lost labor there.

Tigre was an admirable character, really. There were not many ways you could avoid being eaten by the Tupinambás. Shitting yourself, literally, is the usual European tactic, and it works better than pissing yourself, though that works pretty well too. Take Hans Staden, for example, he shat and pissed himself and wasn't eaten. But then they keep him as a pet and treated him like the shit and piss he produced in order to avoid being eaten in the first place. By levitating, Tigre managed to be kept as a spiritual adviser and treated like an avatar. He wouldn't think twice about eating one of the Tupinambás in the tribe, though, were he in a position to do so. Even the more skeptical of us in the ship believed that all the Goitacás, not just Tigre, ate human flesh because they found it tasty. The Goitacás are ferocious, you see. So much so that even armed Portuguese soldiers were afraid of them. They could swim and run faster than any of the peoples the Portuguese had had contact with. And we had had contact with many peoples. Nobody could beat the Goitacás on their own ground; not the Europeans, not other Indians. Henrique Lobos, the bravest man I've ever known, said not even the Jesuits would be able to exterminate the Goitacás. He was almost right. Smallpox played a big role in it. But this happened so many years later, generations later, and I don't like to talk like that, ahead of myself, because it makes me feel so old. Tigre himself was old then, in 1531, but it was easy to see he had been a strong man. When I saw him he was blind. I saw his toothless gums and was able to imagine how his teeth might have been strong enough to tear through flesh, and how his arms might have been strong enough to crush a skull, but I couldn't imagine him actually killing people and eating them. He had that serene look very old people and sleeping babies have. A harmless look. His toothless speech was so strange that I doubt the Tupinambás actually understood much of it. I think they had stopped understanding him a long time ago. Whatever he said, some shaman or other interpreted in a crazy way and the rest of them accepted it. That's why the Tupinambás in Guanabara Bay were acting so crazy. You say they were Guaranis, not Tupinambás, and maybe that's true, maybe that's why they weren't acting like Tupinambás. But whatever you say, I still think Tigre didn't actually tell that girl to do what she did, maybe no one told her to do it, maybe she just did it because she thought that it was the right thing to do.

That's why the parrots were shouting "akâ" like old women, cheering the Tupinambá who came to the ship to reclaim Niño de Juan's head. No one knew anything about her. We hadn't seen her before, and we had been in Guanabara Bay for about three months before she climbed on board. Some said she was related to Niño de Juan. Maybe she was his stepsister. All that the men really knew was what they could see: that she was the most wonderful woman in the world, and that her glistening body was still dripping the Atlantic Ocean on the deck when, in a masturbatory gesture, she reached for the long rusty nail hidden inside her cunt, making the parrots go berserk in frenzied screaming, and causing the abundant body hair of all sailors present to stand on end. We saw that she was going to kill Martim and we wouldn't be able to stop her.

—

Dieguito had never seen a naked woman before, but he said he could tell, from the sound the Tupinambá made when swimming, that she had petite breasts and no clothes on. You see, he had a more acute sense of smell, and hearing, than any animal in the world, so he knew the Tupinambá was either ovulating or holding a rusty nail inside her vagina.

You have to understand, of course, that the rusty nail she had was not her own, and that Dieguito had never seen a naked woman, in all of his 38 years of existence, because he had been blind until that day. So when he miraculously began to see things, in the exact moment the Tupinambá landed her left foot on the deck, the only reason he knew what he was seeing was a naked woman, drenched with the Atlantic, was because he had heard her swimming and had smelt her climbing on board.

You laugh certain laughs. ...maybe you're right, maybe there's never been any magic in the world, maybe it's just my memory fantasticating all that happened. You, with your little scribbles about History, you can doubt all you want. I can see that if you were one of the men traveling with Martim Afonso, you would be siding with the more skeptical of us, like Father Conselheiro—who was, of course, an atheist immune to all known sexual diseases. But his manners were so catholic, like his speech, that I doubt there has ever been a priest so eloquent. Not even Father Vieira, whom you like to read, was a match for him, and definitely, in my spoken history, no one has converted more Indians, Africans, Muslims and Jews than Conselheiro. His public persona was more Catholic than St. Augustine in his later years, but privately he didn't believe in any god he had heard or read about, and he also loved deviant sexual practices. He was, in that aspect, like the Pope. Father Conselheiro was an ageless man, always active and ready to convert infidels. He would have converted all indigenous tribes in Brazil, if only they had been in the habit of wearing clothes. Naked as they were, Father Conselheiro forgot all his sermons and proceeded to whiten their future offspring by having sex with all the natives of childbearing age. In the first few days after we arrived, he was almost certainly copulating with ten different women a day. His great breakthrough, though, came one day when he found a hollow tree, leaning but still standing. He climbed up a few branches, found a way in through a big hole, not too distant from the ground. After dislodging a marsupial that lived in the tree, he discovered that he could stay and rest snugly inside the trunk, protected from the elements. Being such a virile man, he made a small perforation in the trunk and, there, inserted his erection. I don't know how the native women found out about it, but soon there were hundreds of women queuing up near the tree, taking turns to enjoy the new variety of mushroom they had found. Very firm and colorful. Women everywhere in Brazil heard about this biological phenomenon and traveled great distances to get to it. It's impossible to calculate how many women he enjoyed in this way, during the time he was missing, presumed dead; but I firmly believe no one in the world ever had as many different partners in a lifetime as Father Conselheiro had in just over two months. He came back as naked and thin as an earthworm, crawling, with a strange smell of flowers and jacaranda; his penis limp, disfigured, and useless; his face pure happiness. He would be happier, he later confessed, if only he could have the woman who stared Martim Afonso de Sabrosa in the eye, without a touch of fear, with a nail hidden inside her.

The nail the Tupinambá brought with her had been taken, by someone else, from the Trinidad, the ship captained by Magellan. Do you mean to say that I'm not the first one to divulge this? You say that Pigafetta mentions it in his account of the first voyage around the world? That may well be. Martim Afonso and I once met Pigafetta, before setting out to sail around the world going east, but he didn't mention anything about women and nails. All I know is what Vasco Garcia Galego told me: that, back in 1519, a native woman climbed on board the Trinidad ready to offer sex in exchange for any metal object, but when she saw a nail lying around she just took it, stored it somewhere in the nether regions, and jumped out of the boat.

It couldn't have been the same Tupinambá woman, unless she, like me, doesn't age. It's very possible as well, that Magellan's men had taken parrots inside their ships, to take back to Europe, like we did. But their parrots wouldn't have been screaming "akâ," when native women climbed on board, because the son of João Lopes de Carvalho, Niño de Juan, was still alive and well, his head was still attached to his body. I hope Magellan's men didn't take parrots inside the ships. Garcia Galego certainly didn't mention eating parrots when they were starving in the Pacific Ocean. You see this parrot here? It's an old, old parrot: its feathers are losing color, it can no longer fly, but it tells me things. Magellan and his men would have certainly eaten lovely birds like these when they were starving in the Pacific, or before that, when they were starving in the Atlantic.

It's a great shame that Magellan died in Mactan, before completing his journey. He wanted to show the power of the Spanish to Lapulapu, one of the important leaders in the islands of the Philippines. He should have stuck to his roots and been more Portuguese then, and forgotten Lapulapu's offence to the King of Spain. Why should Magellan care? But what João Lopes de Carvalho did was worse still. After Magellan's death, he took over the last remaining ship of the Armada Moluca, and made one mistake after another. He even abandoned his own son in Borneo, who ended up having his head cut off, desiccated, and later sold to Martim Afonso de Sabrosa, almost ten years later, for a bargain. A bargain in terms, that is, because it later cost his life. Maybe Martim Afonso should never have bought the head of Niño de Juan from the Dayaks. Maybe he should never have brought the head back to the place where it came from. Maybe he should have given the head back to the boy's mother, when the Indians asked him to. If he had done it, he would even have gained extra respect from the Tupinambá, they might even consider trading things with the Portuguese again, despite the deal they had with Pierre le Bastard and the rest of the French pirates. But then, if he had given the head back, the most wonderful creature in the world would not have killed him so gracefully.

Dieguito would have warned us all about the nail the woman was carrying inside her. He always warned us of danger. But he claimed he had lost his special smelling and hearing abilities the minute he started to see, which was the same minute she landed her left foot on the deck. Dieguito knew what our beards smelt like, but he had never seen them. He was completely disoriented, because he couldn't associate the visions he now had, with the smells he used to have. But we think that what really disconcerted him most of all, was that the first thing he ever saw, when he became capable of seeing, was the woman.

She was so wonderful, in pulling the nail out of her vagina, that Father Conselheiro fainted, very catholically. She was so sensual, in moving past the sailors, that the pilot, Pedro Paes, never again had intercourse with men. So breathtaking, in her stabbing motion, that Martim couldn't say "I love you," before she pierced his jugular and watched him bleed to death while we all watched her.

After she took the desiccated head of Niño de Juan, spat on Martin's dead face, and jumped out of the ship, the parrots went quiet, and two able seamen and a gunner tried to follow her and drowned. They washed up on the shore a few days later: blue and bloated, with little crabs in their ears. The Italian caulker, Giovanni, gouged his own eyes out because he wanted that woman to be the last thing he ever saw. He closed his eyes and felt for his knife, and carefully punctured his eyes, eyelids still shut. That was quite lucky, really, because he began to predict the future very accurately as a result. He said if we stayed much longer in those parts, we'd all be killed. But the men, the ones still living, wanted to stay there forever, wait for the woman to come back. They hoped and dreamed she would stare them down, bleed them dead, and spit on their faces.

Mystery Meat: Curious Cases of Unintentional Cannibalism

Pamela Siska

Although not very well known, "Taboo" by Geoffrey Household is one of the most memorable treatments of cannibalism in fiction. Written in 1938, the tale is atmospheric and suspenseful. But it is more than exciting reading: the story is also thoughtful, touching on some of the moral and psychological issues evoked by this pungent topic: motives for cannibalism, reactions to the breaking of such a strong taboo, questions of profound hunger, atavism, and the depth of human instincts. While all these features make "Taboo" a fine story, I think the reason it has such great impact is because it involves not only intentional cannibalism but also the unwitting consumption of human flesh, what I will call "unintentional cannibalism."

The story begins with Dr. Shiravieff, a psychologist specializing in cases of shell shock in World War One veterans, debating with his friends Romero and Banning the question of whether it is better to keep one's emotions inside or to display them. Romero admires English reserve and suggests that the English are not really cold or unemotional but simply conceal their emotions as a matter of good breeding. Shiravieff counters that while this may be so, keeping emotions inside when they must be displayed, as in the face of a shock, is unhealthy and can cause permanent psychological damage. When Banning roguishly remarks that he has shocked the English and they have shown plenty of emotion, Shiravieff replies that the kind of shock he means is not a flouting of social conventions but confrontation with a "horrid fact:" "It is our horror of breaking a taboo that causes shock. Listen to me. Do either of you remember the Zweibergen case in 1926?" (Household, 261). With this question, he begins to recount his story of that summer in the eastern Carpathians.

Shiravieff travels to Zweibergen for his holiday only to find that his usual shooting box has already been rented, by the

Vaughns—an Englishman and his American wife. He has little contact with them at first, but soon they are drawn together by a series of mysterious disappearances. When first one villager and then another go missing, theories abound: some say the men were murdered; some say they were attacked by wolves, possibly werewolves (after all, it *is* the Carpathians); others speculate that they met with accidents or simply left of their own free will. When a third peasant vanishes, Shiravieff and Vaughn decide to lay a trap for the man or beast responsible for the killings, using themselves as bait. Their plan succeeds: walking down a lonely forest path at night, Shiravieff is attacked from behind by what turns out to be one of the villagers, Josef Weiss. Shiravieff and Vaughn pursue Weiss, following him through a dry channel under a sulphur spring and into an underground cave. They kill Weiss, but the horror does not end there. Beyond Weiss's body, the men spot a hole in the cave wall, leading to an underground passage. At the end of the passage, a crude ladder leads up to a cottage. In the cottage, they discover "a table in the center of the room with long knife on it" and evidence of Weiss's cannibalistic indulgence.

Days before the gruesome discovery, in a conversation about hunger, Weiss revealed that he had been a prisoner of war in World War One. Forgotten behind the walls of a fortress, he and his fellow prisoners were "reduced to very desperate straits indeed" (Household, 268). His experience was not an uncommon one: in *The Cannibal Within*, Lewis Petrinovich writes of the "many brutal instances in which political prisoners were starved to the point where they engaged in cannibalism" (188). Although cannibalism among POWs is associated most readily with the Russian, German, and Japanese camps of World War Two, it was also prevalent in World War One. In fact, the situation was sufficiently dire as to be covered by *The New York Times:* the May 23, 1918 "Topics of the Times" column reported on cannibalism in Austria among prisoners of war ("Starvation"). Weiss's experience apparently "left a kink in the poor devil's mind," (Household, 278) in Shiravieff's words. His cannibalistic tendencies lay dormant for years, but when he discovered the dry spring channel beneath his cottage, Weiss realized he could satisfy his "secret desire" for human flesh without fear of being caught.

If "Taboo" ended with the revelation of Weiss's deeds, the story would be horrifying enough. But what follows, what Shiravieff calls the "extra horror," is what makes it so very compelling. When Weiss's abattoir is discovered, a rumor spread that what he had been selling around the village, as venison, was human flesh. In fact, a joint of "venison" was what the Vaughns served Shiravieff the first time they asked him to dinner. Vaughn believes the rumor but feels that "looking at the affair calmly it did not matter; that no one could have known; the best thing was to forget" (Household, 279). Despite his attempts to calm her, his wife Kyra is appalled by their unwitting consumption of human flesh and breaks down, crying all night long, and in this way purging herself of the horror and her feelings of guilt. Vaughn, who seemed to take the matter in stride, breaks down years later when the suppressed revulsion and shock come back to him in the form of a distaste for meat that he can not understand: "he could not think why," Shiravieff recalls, as he reiterates his point about the danger of suppressing strong emotion: "Shock had lain hidden in him for ten years and then had claimed its penalty." (Household, 280)

"Taboo" is a work of fiction, but do such things *really* happen? Under what circumstances could someone eat human flesh and not be aware of it? This scenario is not as fantastic as it seems. All it requires is a third party, a mediator, between the eaten and the eater. Cases of "unintentional cannibalism" are more common than might be imagined.

Survival cannibalism during wartime is a well-known phenomenon. But do the straitened circumstances of war ever lead to *unintentional* cannibalism? In *Cannibalism: From Sacrifice to Survival* Hans Askenasy highlights a small footnote in the sweeping story of the Franco-Prussian War: "In 1871, when the Germans encircled Paris, a French butcher shop on the island of Saint Louis sold human flesh. This was not known until much later, after the siege had been lifted; by that time the shop has achieved a great reputation for the quality of its meat." (Askenasy, 69)

In the years following World War One, several famous cases of unintentional cannibalism unfolded in Germany, and one wonders whether they were Household's inspiration for "Taboo." In *Before the Deluge: A Portrait of Berlin in the 1920's*, historian Otto Friedrich reports that in 1924, shopkeeper Karl Denke, living in the town of Münsterberg, was found in possession of barrels "filled with smoked human flesh, a case full of bones, and a number of pots of human lard." (Petrinovich, 193) Also found were Denke's notebooks, in which he had meticulously recorded the dates of his over two dozen murders, along with the weight of each of his victims. Apparently he needed to procure his meat in volume: he had been very successful at selling his "smoked pork." (Petrinovich, 193)

Berlin saw other cases of unintentional cannibalism during this period. In 1924, Fritz Haarmann sold "attractively packaged tinned meats labeled pork or veal on the Black Market." (Petrinovich, 193) It was suspected that these tins contained something other than what their labels indicated after Haarmann confessed to murder and nothing but the bones of his numerous victims were found. Yet another enterprising cannibal in Weimar Berlin was former butcher Carl Grossmann, who, in 1921, sold at the city's train station frankfurters made from the ground flesh of his victims, primarily young women. (Tannahill, 242; Askenasy, 31-32)

Germany was not the only place where post-World War One cannibalism flourished. In *The Famine in Soviet Russia*, Harold Fisher reports that in the early 1920's there were "seven cases in which murder was committed and the bodies were sold. In these ...cases the flesh was disguised in the form of sausages and sold on the open market." (Petrinovich, 177) In another Russian case of the same era, when police made inquiries at a market where the head of a murder victim had been found, they learned that the killer had sold the victim's dismembered body to another man, who sold it in the market In response to this discovery, the city issued an order "forbidding the sale of meatballs, cutlets, and all forms of hashed meats." (Petrinovich, 177)

Instances of unintentional cannibalism have occurred in recent times too. In *Stiff: The Curious Lives of Human Cadavers*, Mary Roach draws upon Ken Ray Chong's *Cannibalism in China* to relate the story of a Beijing couple who, in 1985, murdered a young man, cooked him up, and then gave some of the meat to their neighbors, "telling them it was camel meat." (Roach, 237) Interestingly, the couple admitted that, á la Josef Weiss, they were trying to satisfy a lingering taste for human meat that had developed during wartime. (Roach, 237) In 1993 the *Arizona Star Daily* picked up from the AP news wire this story from Moscow:

> *A family preparing a holiday dinner became worried when a bullet was found in what was thought to be beef, a newspaper said yesterday. They were sickened at the news from police: They had been preparing human flesh.* Moskovskii Komsomolets *reported that the unidentified Moscow family bought the slab of meat at a state store in Moscow and put it in the freezer. They pulled it out on June 12, [1993,] Russian Independence Day, and began cutting, the newspaper said. When the family dog was offered a piece of the strangely colored meat, "The dog sniffed it, whimpered pitifully and left," the account said. Then the family found the bullet and called the police."* (Askenasy, 36).

These are some of the better-documented cases. Scores of similar stories, from all over the globe, can be found by searching the Internet. But most such stories are apocryphal: they are nearly impossible to verify—or refute—because they give only sketchy details, often lacking basic information such as dates and place names.

When delving into cases of unintentional cannibalism, it is hard to escape the nagging question of whether any of the apparently unwitting diners had any inkling about what they were buying and eating. The Russian family's dog, with its keen sense of smell, was able to tell, but should humans be able to? In "Taboo" Kyra Vaughn blames her cook, who actually purchased the "venison" from Weiss. She wants to dismiss the cook, believing that she should have known better, but her husband defends the woman, arguing that there was no way she could have known, being an ignorant peasant woman and "not an anatomist." (Household, 279) Vaughn's point seems a valid one. It is reasonable to contend that a slab of human meat looks very much like any other chunk of meat. We can tell beef from pork from lamb, but if we are not expecting something out of the ordinary, why would it even enter our minds? Unless we had some reason, we would not suspect that the cutlet we just bought was human flesh any more than we would think it was, say, zebra meat. And if the meat is ground up or potted or made into frankfurters, surely it becomes impossible to tell. If appearance is not a guide, can taste be used as an indicator? By all accounts, human flesh is quite sweet and tastes very much like pork ("long pig"), so taste is not a conclusive factor, especially when the meat is seasoned, as it likely would be if potted or made into frankfurters or sausages.

It seems safe to assume that those who bought the meat products had no hint of their origin and would therefore have been horrified to learn the truth. A glimpse into one city's response to such a nightmarish revelation is offered by novelist Vicki Baum, who lived in Hanover at the time of Haarmann's crimes: "When Haarmann made a full confession there was much silent shock, frightened inspection of hidden larders, some discreet vomiting, and a general throwing way of expensive potted-meat jars." (Askenasy, 139) But because, in Hanover and elsewhere, the purchasers of the potted meat, frankfurters, "smoked pork," etc. were anonymous, we can only speculate about their individual reactions. Perhaps somewhere, on the pages of moldering journals or yellowing letters, faded ink records the feelings of German or Russian men and women when they found out, after reading the newspaper or overhearing whispered rumors in the marketplace, what they'd eaten for supper.

In trying to imagine their reactions, we may search for analogous scenarios in which other taboos are broken unwittingly. The first to come to mind is *Oedipus Rex*, but are there real-life parallels on a scale less grand than that of Greek tragedy? The annals of crime include poisoning cases in which poisoners have engineered their murders so that the poison was actually administered, unknowingly, to the victim by another's hand. In these cases, the intermediary obviously assumes no legal blame, even though he may certainly be wracked with guilt when the facts come to light. But the obvious difference in cases of unintentional cannibalism is that the taboo act does not harm another person: those whose flesh is consumed are already dead. A closer parallel would be the unintentional violation of religiously prescribed dietary restrictions. Even though the transgression is unintentional, the eater would surely feel distraught and possibly even guilty.

Like many other "dark" or outré subjects, unintentional cannibalism evokes revulsion mingled with fascination. We thrill to read about unintentional cannibalism because we believe that it will never happen to us. But can we be so sure? Do we know exactly what is in every packaged and prepared food that we buy? And how would we react if it did happen to us? On Mister Poll, a web site featuring polls on topics ranging from sports to religion to music, a 2002 question in the category of Controversy/Morality asks respondents whether they would be upset if they went to someone's house and were served human meat but were not told until after the meal. Of the 907 respondents, 49% answered "Yes," 16% answered "No," and 7% answered "I Don't Know." The remaining 25% selected the fourth response: "I eat people all the time." Perhaps these results need to be taken with a grain of salt.

WORKS CITED

Askenasy, Hans. *Cannibalism: from Survival to Sacrifice.* Amherst, NY: Prometheus Books, 1994.

Household, Geoffrey. "Taboo." *Great Tales of Terror and the Supernatural.* Ed. Phyllis Cerf Wagner and Herbert Wise. New York: Modern Library, 1944.

"Human Meat." Mister Poll. 9 May 2002. 3 July 2005. <http://www.misterpoll.com>.

Petrinovich, Lewis. *The Cannibal Within*. New York: Aldine de Gruyter, 2000.

Roach, Mary. *Stiff: The Curious Lives of Human Cadavers*. New York: W.W. Norton, 2003

"Starvation Leads to Cannibalism." *New York Times*. 23 May 1918. *New York Times Historical Archive*. Proquest. MIT Libraries, Cambridge, MA. 3 July 2005. <http//www.nytimes.com/archives>

Tannahill, Reay. *Flesh and Blood: A History of the Cannibal Complex*. New York: Stein and Day, 1975.

ROAST FALLOPIAN TUBES
Alice Mills

The camel incident I blame on Neil. All I asked for was a meal of camel-meat, and he had a whole week to find some in the shops and cook it for me; you could not expect me to be waddling up the supermarket aisles in my condition, could you? I knew there were problems when he came home later and later every night, even took a day off work and went to town on the train. So on Friday he presented the grand meal, camel steak with rice and cauliflower, but I knew it was all a lie. I'd been in the kitchen and spotted the plastic wrapper, plain old ordinary porterhouse steak. I ate it up and said nothing, pretended to ooh and ah over its flavor, its tenderness. But all the while I was chewing at it—gristly it was and the cauliflower underdone—I could have cheerfully sunk my teeth into Neil. But all that comes later.

At any rate, there is no way I can be blamed for the camel week, or rather the non-camel week. And I had done so well up till then. I always say it is important to keep your word, and so far I'd honored every word on my list, even the spiders. To tell you the truth, I was secretly worried about the spiders. It was easy enough to get hold of the first item on the list, bacteria: all I had to do was choose a puddle in the garden and drink a bit of it. Of course it was easier for me to get up and down then, no problem at all, and it was so easy it barely counted as eating. Perhaps, though, I should really have looked at it through a microscope just to make absolutely sure there really were bacteria in the water; I still worry about that. It is so important to keep your word, and if anyone challenged me about the bacteria, I wouldn't have a leg to stand on, so to speak.

It was the spiders that seriously worried me, though. It seemed such an easy week, as easy as the ants week where all I needed was a warm day and a block of chocolate. So I acted like an idiot and waited until the Friday, the last possible day of the week, and suddenly they had all gone into hiding. All I could find was two skinny spiders and one of them only had seven legs. It would have been all right if my list had said "spider," no problem, but like an idiot I had written down "spiders," so spiders plural it had to be. Do two spiders without their full complement of legs actually count as spiders, plural? Or did I mess up that week as well? And I can't blame anyone else for the spider problem. Perhaps I should have specified one of those big fat tarantulas—then I would really have known I was eating a spider. Those two skinny items tasted of nothing at all, wrapped up in a slice of bread, barely counts as eating. But then again, I would definitely have failed the spider week if it had been tarantula on the menu. Be grateful for small mercies, I say.

One of which is the nice way the neighbors took the disappearance of their cat. It was a bugger to catch. I was getting quite clumsy by then and not much good at running, and it gave me some very nasty scratches. Luckily they were up my arm and I just threw the blouse in the garbage. Neil did not seem to notice anything wrong with me. Of course, around that time he was getting truly obsessed with my stomach, kept putting his hand on it to feel the child kick, said he could hear its heart beating when he pressed his ear against me. That was a good week, once the cat was safely in the freezer waiting for Friday lunch.

Just as well I hadn't planned on serving cat for dinner. It tasted truly horrible and I couldn't keep it down. I don't see how anyone could be expected to digest all that furry stuff, and I kept throwing up all afternoon. So I took the remains of the casserole down the street as soon as I could, just in case Neil felt peckish and started poking around in the fridge, and stuffed it in the garbage bin outside the shops. It was then that I felt better about the spiders. Nobody could expect me to eat a whole cat, so the same should apply to every item on the list. Honor would be satisfied if I just had a plateful—but it had to be a real plateful, no tip-of-the-tongue stuff, otherwise the dog week would have been much easier.

I blame the dog for that week going wrong. It did not have to struggle so hard. All I wanted was a chunk out of its leg, so that I could say I had well and truly eaten dog, but the way it kicked in my arms, I ended up with a lapful of blood and a dead dog, not what I had planned at all. And then I had to make up a story to tell Neil about how I'd slipped while I was cutting up the meat for the stew and the knife had gone into the dog by mistake. The problems of keeping your word, who'd have thought it would be so difficult? Then Neil was so upset about the dog that he didn't want any dinner. Just as well, really, that meant I was totally confident I had eaten dog, once I had got through the whole potful.

I blame the whole thing, actually, on those people we went on holiday with in Vietnam. It was a mistake going on a coach tour, I see that now, gave them a chance to start making personal comments about me, calling me "Dinah, the girl who eats everything." Just because I was a bit more adventurous than they were, you would think they had never been to a restaurant and seen a menu with anything more exciting on it than hamburger. So when they saw me eating snails, and the next night I tried the sea-urchin, and they just had to say, "Dinah will eat anything" and like an idiot I said yes. So that's why I put together my list, to keep my word to myself that I would eat everything. It's a bit silly, I know, but you have to keep your word, and by next week I'll have worked through the whole list—apart from the camel, blame Neil for that one—and honor will be satisfied.

The trouble with the list is the last item. It was all very well listing bacteria and worm, they can be found any day of the week, and mouse and lizard were easy enough because of the weather, though it is getting cooler these days and the lizard took a lot of finding. But fallopian tubes are another thing again. I've been worrying about them a lot, not helped by Neil confessing about the camel. "Di," he said (I hate it when he calls me that), "could you forgive me if I told you I couldn't get hold of camel, but I promise you, once we can travel again, we'll take a trip to the desert and you can eat camel to your heart's content." I dare say he is secretly thinking that all this fuss is about being pregnant and wanting strange foods, but it is not. I blame it all on the coach trip. It wasn't my fault that we went to a restaurant in the middle of nowhere, which had roast fallopian tubes on the menu. I can't imagine why I didn't notice; perhaps I was distracted by the prospect of spiny anteater with chips. So nothing would have happened if they hadn't started on at me again, once we were back on the bus. "How come you didn't try the roast fallopian tubes?" they had to say, "I wonder whose tubes they were, would you eat them if they came from a person?" And by then it was too late, the coach was driving off and once I'd said of course I would eat roast fallopian tubes, there was no way of going back and keeping my word on the spot. And then it was not on the menu anywhere else. I looked and looked. That is the problem with being honest and honorable, once you have said something, you absolutely have to do it. And I had said that I was the person who would eat anything, specifically fallopian tubes. Hence the last item on my list.

Roast human it had to be, and the list was really only a way of working up to it; it was a bit much to contemplate eating human parts right there and then, without some kind of lead-up. Of course I didn't list every possible item that I might eat, otherwise I'd never have come to the point, I mean, when you consider the number of different insect there are, I could be eating one a week till kingdom come and that does not sound to me like keeping my word, more like putting off the real challenge. If I were to be truly honest, I'd have to admit that the first version of the list skirted around the problem of fallopian tubes. For weeks and weeks, I'm ashamed to say, I thought I had it all worked out like child's play. All I had to do was wait until the birth was over and then eat the placenta. That way I would keep my word, eat human flesh, and all my problems would be over.

Then I started to fret about it. Those people on the coach had specifically mentioned roast fallopian tubes, and like an idiot I had said I would eat them, given another chance. So I was committed and placenta just would not do. It will have to be the baby, like it or not, and I'm also worried about giving birth no later than the end of next week, otherwise the list is all wrong again. I think no one can blame me if the last item happens a little late, under the circumstances. But I haven't yet worked out how I'm going to get away from Neil; he's going to take a couple of weeks off work to look after us, what a nuisance. And I'm still not sure exactly where fallopian tubes are, so I intend to roast the whole baby, minus arms and legs of course. Things will work themselves out, they always do, I think it will fit into my big roasting dish, and I'll be able to keep my word and then I can relax. Roast fallopian tubes eaten, honor satisfied.

Only I've had a really bothersome thought. What happens if the baby is a boy?

ONE MAN'S MUTI…

Terence FitzSimons

The red dust was pumping through every gap in the Citroën's bodywork as the car bounced over the corrugations in the dirt road. Dacy never liked taking periodical court at Nkai and, as the court roll was a heavy one he, would probably have to stay overnight at the Police Camp. The car radio crackled and faded.

"See if you can tune that in," said Dacy to Jerry Cheda. The court interpreter fiddled with the radio for a moment.

"I think that's the best reception you'll get, sir."

"I'm not surprised," sniffed Dacy. "Nothing works out in this part of the world. What are they on about anyway?"

Cheda listened for a moment. "It's a report about the Lancaster House talks."

"Oh, turn it off. Nothing's going to come of that." The two men sat in silence for a while. The car would occasionally slew sideways and crab along the road, kicking up even greater clouds of dust. "Well, if there are any terrs up in those kopjies, they're certainly going to know we're here," said Dacey, nodding to the line of hills away to his right. He glanced across at Cheda. "You ready for trouble?" The interpreter hefted the Harrison .410 shotgun on his lap. "Good man," smiled Dacy. "But make sure you shoot that thing out your window, I don't want you firing across my face." Dacy took a moment to glance at Cheda. "You know, the art is not to hit anyone…it's just to scare 'em off. Let 'em know we are armed."

"Yes, sir, I am aware of that," replied Cheda, stiffly.

"Good," grunted Dacey, and patted the Taurus .38 in his shoulder holster. "There's a turnoff somewhere up here. One way's off to Silobela, and we go left to Nkai."

—

The police station and courthouse were part of a scattering of wood and metal buildings that formed the administrative centre for the local native communal lands. The green and white Rhodesian flag flying from a pole in the middle of a dusty square confirmed the location's official status. Inspector Don Milton headed the police unit at Nkai. He was a beefy man, in his early thirties. It was his declared intention still to be single at sixty, and to have reached the rank of chief inspector—to Milton's way of thinking, modest and achievable objectives. He came from his office to greet Darcy as the dust-reddened Citroën pulled to a halt. "Good trip from Gwelo?" he asked. Dacy motioned to Cheda to take the case, containing his robe and a change of clothes, while he took the shotgun from the front seat, at the same time vainly dusting his once-white shirt.

"Good trip? You're joking, of course," he scowled. "When was that road last graded?"

"As bad as that, was it? Well. Public Works aren't going to put a gang out there till the terrorists have moved on or been cleared out." Milton motioned Dacy towards the small wooden shack that served as his office.

"But it's quite in order for a magistrate and his interpreter to provide target practice for 'freedom fighters'!" grumbled Darcy.

"I'll get us some tea," said Milton by way of reply.

Dacy had worked with Milton before. He considered him a common-sense enough prosecutor, though he held reservations about the merits of police prosecutors in general. "They get too close to their cases," was his refrain to the Provincial Magistrate. "Give me a public prosecutor every time."

"We've got a heavy load today. You've come prepared to stay overnight?" asked Milton as he poured the tea.

"Safe to travel by day, when we can be seen—dangerous at night when we can't be spotted!" scoffed Dacy.

"Something like that," smiled Milton "Though the idea is you can see the terrs by day, but you can't see them by night."

"Subtle!" snorted Dacy. "But, what have you got for me today?"

"There is a fair amount of intimidation going on. ZANU have shifted in here, and ZAPU aren't to happy about that, and the locals are being caught in the middle," explained Milton, shuffling through his files. "I've charged the troublemakers under common law, where I can, but there are a number of cases under the Law and Order Maintenance Act. And," he added as an afterthought, "there is an interesting Liquor Act matter."

"All right. Cheda has probably got things organised in the court. Let's start."

"Before we go in, can you give me a minute?" asked Milton. "I've got a situation involving one of my constables."

"Don't talk to me if you're thinking of charging him," countered Dacy. "If we discuss any potential prosecution I couldn't take the case, and your lad would most likely finish up being sent back to Gwelo."

"Maybe," conceded Milton, "but I'd like to hear what you think of the facts."

"Well, I'm staying overnight," said Dacy. He glanced at his watch "I can make the time."

—

The story was straightforward. Constable Mika Ncube had been out on two-day patrol when, to use his phrase, he had "received information." A family at one of the local kraals had been giving food to some of the ZANU terrorists—Ncube used the term "boys in the bush." Ncube wanted to know where the "boys" were located, and when they likely to come back. The family expresses great surprise that Ncube would think for a moment that they would have anything to do with ZANU, or for that matter, ZAPU. They were always happy to help the police but, with regard this matter, they knew nothing. They were a simple family, father mother and son, with a mealie patch to harvest, and a few cows to tend. What would they know about politics?

"I am taking this boy with me," Ncube announced to the startled parents, slipping handcuffs onto their fifteen-year-old son's wrists. "You will tell me what I want to know," he said, as he pushed the youth through the gate of the kraal. "You will tell me." Ncube had been with the British South Africa Police for twenty years, and he was keen to make sergeant before he retired.

The couple trotted after Ncube and his captive, protesting their ignorance of any ZANU presence. "You will tell me," called Ncube, as they gave up and slowly made their way back to the kraal.

A day later Constable Ncube returned to the kraal. The parents cautiously came out of their hut. "What do you want to tell me?" demanded Ncube.

"We have nothing to tell you," protested the father. "And where is our son?"

Ncube ignored the question. "Bring me a drink of water." The mother scuttled away to do his bidding. "I have your son," said Ncube to the father. "What have you to tell me?" The man shook his head and remained silent. "Tomorrow, you shall seen then," announced Ncube and left the kraal as the mother returned with a mug of water.

The following day Ncube returned in the mid-morning, carrying a small Hessian sack slung over his shoulder.

"Now, old man, what have you to tell me?"

The father stood mute, his wife at his side.

"I thought so. Even if you had told me, it would have been too late," continued Ncube confusingly. "You have made me wait too long." He shook open the sack and took out a shank of cooked meat and bit into it. "Your son now only has one leg," he told the couple.

—

"Bloody hell!" exclaimed Dacy.

"Well, Constable Ncube got the information," said Milton. "And we cleaned out a nasty little nest of terrs." Dacy was speechless. "Relax!" smiled Milton. "It was a leg of goat."

"I don't care what it was," snapped Dacy. "That was unforgivable conduct. It was…it was…" he struggled for a word. "Gross!"

"Needless to say, I've given him a dressing-down," said Milton calmly. "But I can't find an offence here—to misrepresent yourself as a cannibal isn't against the law as I read it." Milton paused. "I must say, I was taken by his inventiveness."

"Don't be so bloody glib," retorted Dacy. "I view your man's misconduct in a very serious light. There will be something in the Miscellaneous Offences Act to cover it."

"Well, I was happy just to give him a bollicking," shrugged Milton. "But, if you want to take it further…"

"Indeed, I do," snapped Dacy. "This is going to the Public Prosecutor in Gwelo."

"Maybe I shouldn't have mentioned it to you—just kept it internal," suggested Milton.

"Oh, I'm quite sure there are many things it would be better I didn't know. Now, let's get on with the rest of the day."

—

The flimsy plasterboard used to line the ceiling did little to insulate the courtroom from the throbbing heat. Dacy had donned a fresh shirt and slacks, and had his gown about his neck, to disguise the fact that he wasn't wearing a tie or jacket. He was certain none of the accused could have given a tinker's cuss how he was dressed; but he had his standards. As the day wore on the courtroom became stifling. Fortunately, most of the cases were dispatched on pleas of guilty and no evidence needed to be called. However, the Law and Order cases proved troublesome. The accused defended themselves vigorously and interrupted proceedings with shouts of "Viva ZANU!" and "Viva the Patriotic Front!"

By evening Dacy, Milton and a near exhausted Cheda, were all becoming testy. Dacy shuffled through his papers "How many more cases have we, Mister Prosecutor?"

"Just one, Your Worship," said Milton. "A charge under the Liquor Act. Illegal distilling."

"Put the charge, Mister Cheda," directed Dacy. Cheda did so. The accused was an old stooped old man, who, despite the melting heat, clutched an animal skin cloak about his shoulders. He nodded as Cheda read the details of the charge in Shona. "How do you plead?" asked Dacy.

"I made the muti," answered the accused, through the interpreter. "Yes, I made this medicine."

"How do we know it's a distillate, Mister Prosecutor?"

Milton fumbled under the prosecutor's table, and produced a four-foot length of wood with a narrow metal pipe nailed onto it. "This, Your Worship, is the still," he announced. "Pot with the mash attached to this end," he indicated. "Fire lit underneath it, and distillate out this end." He bent down again and picked up two bottles of clear liquid. "And this is the final produce."

"Yes, that is my muti," offered the accused.

"I'll take that as a plea of 'guilty'," said Dacy, making the appropriate entry on the charge-sheet.

"May I have my muti back?" asked the accused.

"It may be medicine to you," responded Dacy with a smile, brightening up now that the day's proceedings were almost at an end. "But it's an illicit distillate as far as the law is concerned."

"But I am an nganga," protested the old man, through the interpreter, "and this is very special muti."

Dacy was amused by the display of persistence. "Well, as a medicine man you should be able to afford a $10 fine, or in default of payment, thirty days imprisonment with labour. And the still, and the...muti, are confiscated. Do you need time to pay?" The old man pulled a wad of banknotes from under his cloak. "This court is adjourned," announced Dacy, standing and bowing to Milton.

"Silence in court!" called Cheda.

—

Sunset had not provided any noticeable relief from the heat of the day. A generator putted away at the back of the camp, providing power for the lights, the ancient Frigidaire and a creaking electric fan, located in the canteen. Some of the European Patrol Officers were gathered around the bar counter, quaffing cold Castle lager. Dacy and Milton had been left alone at a table near the ineffective fan. They were drinking brandy and dry ginger ale.

"That old fellow was interesting," remarked Dacy. "One of the old school ngangas. That was a monkey cape he was wearing, wasn't it?"

"Yes," agreed Milton, sipping at his drink. "Probably could have got him under the Wild Life Protection Act for that."

"You wouldn't have thought a primitive pipe get-up like that would have produced anything drinkable." Dacy was beginning to feel relaxed. A few stiff brandies were his usual way of dealing with a tiring day.

"That stuff, drinkable?" scoffed Milton.

"Why not? I have some friends who swear by the native medicines."

"You're not serious," countered Milton. The brandy seemed to be making him cranky rather than carefree.

"Well, we could see for ourselves." Dacy went to an open window and called out to Cheda, who was on the stoep, chatting and drinking beer with some constables. "Jerry, nip over to the courtroom and bring me back one of the exhibits from that last case; the Liquor Act." Cheda put down his beer. "Just one of the bottles." Dacy returned to the table and drained his drink.

Some moments later Cheda appeared at the window and passed through a rag-stopped bottle of clear liquid. He didn't feel free to enter the patrol officers' mess.

"What do you think?" Dacy held up the bottle for Milton to inspect the liquid. "It's a confiscated exhibit—would you like to help me destroy it?" Dacy was feeling much better after the brandies. He pulled the makeshift 'cork' from the bottle and sniffed. "This smells very sweet. I had poteen once when I was in Ireland; this smells quite like it. Care for a swig?"

Milton raised an eyebrow, but made no reply.

"Well, I'm game, even if you're not," laughed Dacy. He poured a measure into his empty glass and drank it in a gulp. He sat for a moment with his head cocked. "Not bad, would you believe, not bad at all." He poured another shot. "Sure you won't try some?"

"I'm sure," replied Milton stolidly.

This time Dacy sipped at the liquor. "Very sweet indeed. Smooth, you could say; slightly nutty. I wonder what that old fellow's ingredients were." Milton grunted, and took a swig of his brandy. "Do you know?" asked Dacy.

"Yes," answered Milton, putting down his empty glass. "The nganga told me."

"Well?" pressed Dacy.

"Corn, some crushed sunflower, sugar...." Milton paused.

"And..." prompted Dacy.

"...and, minced human foetus. One of the local women had aborted and his muti was brewed specially to prevent that happening again."

Dacy was not at the table to hear the explanation. Watched by Cheda and a gaggle of constable, the magistrate was crouched in the middle of the dusty square, being violently ill.

Milton came slowly to the door of the canteen. He had a fresh glass of brandy in his hand. He raised it in mock salute towards Dacy. "Well," he mused to himself, "he did tell me there were many things it was better he didn't know."

The Economy of Food in Old New Guinea

Gene Santoro

History, like life, is made up of coincidences that sometimes we can lasso into what we like to call sense.

Take our relationship with "primitive" peoples. You know, the ones who don't drive SUVs or stare at other editions of themselves on TV struggling to survive contrived dangers on cellphone-free islands. These sorts of folk don't deal with our tonsured notions of reality; they just try to interpret and survive the proliferating welter of flux and disorientation. They know that Reality Unedited is so not ready for prime time that our very perceptual apparatus insists on cutting its undirected barrage into narratives we can handle. They are Hume-ians.

Here's what you could think of as a Real Story about them.

One day, a soggy batch of luggage washed up in a small cove near one of the villages in Papua New Guinea, as we call it. The natives poked and prodded and ultimately, following a few hours of caution, pulled it apart.

There were piles of axeheads, heaps of (admittedly wet) tobacco, and odd-shaped batches of cloth, which they knew were some form of white man's money and therefore fought over bitterly and with a dab of inevitable bloodshed. This meant the survivors got fatter and richer, which was fine by them. They used the cloth to adorn their carvings and heads, which were the main draw for what white folks came around these parts.

The Asmat tribe figured white people would like their fetishes better if they were dressed like white people. Made sense, right? But they were puzzled (and some were quite annoyed) that none of the buyers ever seemed to recognize any of the heads, even when they were carefully decked out in bits of their own garb. The random and wholesale nature of the whites' head-shopping binges was incomprehensible to the Asmats, but it was also fiercely profitable, at least on paper, and so they hid their bewilderment and bargained for more axeheads and tobacco.

For reasons that escaped the Asmats, whites seemed to have no end of appetite for the heads they shrunk and the carvings they made of wood, their looming totems and animist figurines of gods and warriors. And they paid well for these trophies in two forms the Asmats found very useful. Axeheads and tobacco had changed Asmat life forever. Getting stoked before and after hunting with a new metal weapon was a luxury undreamed of by their forefathers, not to mention their foremothers.

The trade in heads had been booming. One white guy after another, dressed in pith helmet and khaki shorts and hiking boots and waving clipboard and tape recorder, blundered into one or another of the 60 neat and semi-hidden Asmat villages with the droning regularity of mosquitoes. They wanted information. They wanted heads. They wanted carvings. They waved pieces of metal and bolts of cloth and jabbered in jumbles of English, French, German, and Asmat about how they would reward those who brought them what they wanted.

The Asmats, who lived in a world of mud huts, water, and mangrove swamps, thus discovered bit by bit that they were renowned wood carvers, warriors, and ritualistic cannibals.

They also discovered globalization. As trade with anthropologists, curators, and slumming rich Westerners grew, all Asmat boats would rise, their elders in council agreed, and more Asmat bellies would be fuller. No one disagreed. Everyone preferred filling their bellies to becoming filling, even if some were fuller than others. This was one of the tribe's cultural no-brainers.

Every evening of the fullest moon, they gathered round a small hard rectangle that Father Gobeaux had left. When you pressed parts of it, spoke and sang.

A Jesuit missionary, Gobeaux had ultimately given himself to God in the form of a delightfully tempting south Pacific sort of bouillabaisse he'd designed during his four hard proselytizing years among this far-flung flock spread over 10,000 square miles of New Guinea jungle swamp. True, the revamped dish inevitably involved a goodly number of creative ingredient substitutions, but that had been accomplished without lessening, he felt sure, its pungent, savory textures.

Pere Gobeaux's head hung prayerfully over the hut he'd used as a chapel, now converted back into the village smokehouse. As the telltale plume curled from the roof opening, the Asmats never failed to remember him. He had struggled to teach a few of them English and French; sadly, he never knew how well he'd succeeded.

The Asmats responsible for monitoring and translating the periodic emanations of the late Gobeaux's green and white object pressed their ears to its sides. Through the static emerged a few gasping words about a hunt for a lost White Man of Stone. Living in the Stone Age themselves, the Asmats prayed to several tutelary spirits and sharpened their new metal tools, in case he turned up nearby.

Among the Asmat, headhunting was the natural by-product of the fundamental human urge to edit the narrative of history and, in the process, establish proper causality and correct imbalances. Only the deaths of old people and babies were considered normal. Old people passed naturally to the other world, and babies and children under five died either because they had insufficient life force or because they wished to return to the spirit world. So that part of the life-and-death thing was pretty straightforward.

But in Asmat thinking, anyone else died either because they were killed physically or by black magic; the difference there wasn't always apparent, for the Asmat believed there was no such thing as a natural untimely death, especially for local VIPs. The spirits of these unfortunate dead, like Hamlet's dad, would roam in tortured limbo to wreak mischief on the living, until an equal number from among those deemed to have caused their deaths were killed. (This carefully constructed wording, refined by generations of Asmat elders, is even more tortured and vague in their language, leading some Western scholars to speculate that nineteenth-century attorneys must have been shipwrecked in this unlikely spot, gone native, and sired both offspring and the Asmat legal code.)

It's important to note that spirits of women who died in childbirth posed free-floating and hard-to-evade dangers, especially to males. To the Asmat, birth and death balanced the ratios between the seen and the unseen realms of the animist universe—a balance that had to be maintained.

Like Brillat-Savarin, the Asmat believed that you are what you eat; via cannibalism, they harnessed the power of their enemies. The Korowai, the Asmats' nearest neighbors, lived in treetops with pole ladders they pull into their nests at night. Cannibals themselves, the Korowai preferred to eat their own, sharing only grudgingly.

In this animistic universe, the Asmats needed to feel at one with their ancestors. Men wore the skulls of their forefathers, carried them to festivals, used them nightly as pillows. Important headhunters were honored by having their skulls handed down through the generations, lending their owners power and prestige.

Any Asmat smarter than a bamboo cup of mud knew that headhunting was far less dangerous than stalking the ferocious local species of wild pig with a pointed stick and a dog. The rituals surrounding both were equally profound: a boar killer had to carry the slain animal to the public house, where he was given welcome and praise while the animal was ceremonially butchered with the same care as humans. White Western anthropologists speculated that these pigs were treated like people because they, like the Asmat and their neighbors, are nearly black. Whatever. The point is, a pair of tusks worn around the arm conferred the same exalted status as a headhunted human skull.

Few white men traded for pig tusks, however.

When the latest white man arrived—to overstate the manner and tone of his coming, which was as a shapeless bundle of mud washed up on a cove's shoreline—they thought he was already dead. The Asmat living in the nearby village of Otsjanep recognized him from descriptions passed around the villages by the Translators, and began nursing him back to health.

Being primitive, Asmats refused to eat things they could see were unhealthy. When the shaman's mother-in-law with the threatening nose and the sneering eyes had been butchered some moons back, after the metal bird flying over that village dropped a metal egg full of more axeheads, tobacco, and cloth on her while she was roasting one of her nephews in the center of the village, they had ritualistically excised bits that were taboo or disgusting before feasting.

But once he came to, this human stick in tattered khaki and cracked eyeglasses, found floating between two empty gas cans tied together with his leather belt, used his smattering of their dialect and English to convey his identity. He confirmed what the Translators had whispered. This set their minds churning and their mouths watering.

Michael Rockefeller, son of New York State's governor and great-grandson of the dour Puritan who created the modern industrial conglomerate and the oil and banking industries, sat on the board of directors of the Museum of Primitive Art, his father's brainchild. Always looking to diversify, the Rockefellers had realized that if founding and funding the Museum of Modern Art was jolly fun and good publicity, owning two museums could be very great fun and fab PR indeed—especially if they positioned the new one to save primitive art from primitive peoples, who were obviously not to be trusted with it. Ever since they'd reassembled that jigsaw puzzle of European plunder called The Cloisters on New York City's Hudson River banks, the Rockefellers knew that housing art properly for worship of the secular Romantic sort advocated by, say, Matthew Arnold was something Westerners like themselves understood better than anyone else anywhere.

And so they acted accordingly.

Arriving in New Guinea in March 1961, Michael soon found he was just another of the dozens of white Westerners who would someday dream of being played by Harrison Ford—and already, even without Ford (who was only a kid at the time), they were looking over their shoulders for the camera crew as they collected stuff in Irian Jaya. Even a Rockefeller, an alumnus of Harvard, and a 23-year-old anthropological veteran—Michael had spent months in the mountainous interior of western New Guinea with an ethnographic expedition sent out by Harvard's Peabody Museum to study the Ndani peoples—felt that romantic allure of danger and discovery, even if he had few illusions left about Noble Savages or such Frenchified stuff.

This was serious business, the business of Beauty. And the Asmat had an irresistibly hard-to-acquire trove of it, which fired all Michael's keen Rockefeller competitive drive. Besides, this son of Pocantico increasingly envied the natives' rigorous lifestyle.

After a hiatus in the States, where he briefed his family backers, Michael returned to Indonesia in fall 1961. He and anthropologist Rene Wassing and their two native guides all headed for New Guinea's southern coast, where the Asmats lived. He was thrilled to finally contact one of the few Stone Age peoples left on the planet. He couldn't possibly know how zealously the Asmats guarded this status conferred by the White Man: No outsider, for instance, had seen their transistor radio.

Still, the shrewd scion slowly became aware of a certain change in the quality of Asmat life as he canoed from village to village. He suspected that the Asmats' levels of artistry were falling as they churned out imitation artifacts for folks like him. Their skulls these days often looked like they'd been slapped with Colorforms. The once-imposing bis poles got bigger and cruder, as if size was all Westerners understood. They were cheapening their own market, he'd pleaded with growing urgency and despair, and the Asmats had nodded and grinned and clicked their teeth and taken his money and handed over the goods.

In bargaining with the Asmats, Michael had taken advantage of being a Rockefeller. He commanded endless supplies of steel axeheads and tobacco. Since sophisticated LBOs, IPOs, hedged positions, under-the-table rebates, currency fluctuations, stock options and transfers, and offshore incorporation didn't fire the limited Asmat imagination any more than insider advice about their markets did, Michael was forced, like the other whites, to rely on bartering.

Even without their heads buckled to his person, the blood of his forefathers flowed strong in him, which meant he soon wondered how the extremely circumscribed diet of the Asmat might yield an entrepreneurial opening. These hunter-gatherers depended on a single staple: sago, a carbohydrate with all the tantalizing flavor and consistency of the mud it grew in. Since the mud was too poor even to make pottery of, they had neither cooking pots nor stone pit-ovens; all food was roasted over open fires. They bartered for bamboo drinking containers with their better-equipped neighbors in the highlands to the north. The wretches even lacked alcoholic beverages, drinking only the brackish water they collected at low tide.

"The Asmats," Rockefeller wrote thoughtfully in his journal, "live in a world of mud. Even the rivers are grey with it."

But they also smoked like chimneys and delighted in hunting implements that superceded the pointed stick. After showering them with tobacco and axeheads, he wondered, why not up the ante? He'd packed, on the off-chance, a few of the rare cookbooks of the time that dared to navigate beyond the American universe of Jell-O, farm recipes, and casseroles. These would be his new bargaining chips to corner the trade in decorated shrunken heads.

For two months Michael worked the tortured coast of Irian Jaya as if descended from Captain Cook, which probably should have been a warning of sorts. In late November 1961 he, Wassing, and their two guides were battered by a fierce storm 12 miles off the New Guinea coast. Their large trading catamaran, overladen with axeheads and tobacco and clothes, was overturned and smashed. The smaller canoes were battered, then flipped. The two natives dove into the sea and swam desperately for the mouth of the Eilanden River. Michael followed, saying to Wassing, "I think I can make it."

His friend clung to the wreckage and was rescued, while Michael's disappearance grew into the stuff of myth.

Reality was simpler and more devious.

Once he'd dried out enough to return to what passed for consciousness, young Rockefeller's key problem (aside from his broken eyeglasses and shattered legs) was that the Asmats apparently lacked the concept of ransom. He had tried in several tongues to explain that if they got him back to anywhere with a radio or a phone they would be rich beyond their imaginings. They would smile shyly or slyly or incomprehensibly and wave their transistor radio in his direction and look at each other and giggle. It was disconcerting, to say the least.

Still, they treated him well. He seemed to have become a sacred monster. His glasses were cracked but he was otherwise recovering nicely. The old women fed him cackling, the men grinned and traded with him, and the young girls periodically clustered around him with open smiles to bathe and service him. Sometimes he dreamt of Clutch Cargo, an animated cartoon from his childhood where human mouths moved inside expressionless drawn ovals.

Back home, he felt sure, books and movies would be devoted to him. He heard on the radio that his family had spent millions on land and air and sea searches without turning up a thing except questions. Had he gone native? Had he become a cult object or a food source? Was he seen alive on various islands with various women and children? Was his skull hanging on some lucky barterer's belt?

The answers were yes.

The final answer, however, lay in one of his cookbooks. Though the recipe needed some modification, Michael had ultimately been fully inducted into the Asmat tribes as Rockefeller Rockefeller.

BRAIN FOOD

Peter "Toots" Wheat

Frankly—when the invitation arrived—I didn't know what to think of it.

It was probably sent to me because I'd been writing about cannibalism for a decade or so—and a lot of people knew it. Still, it was a total surprise when I opened the envelope. I mean, really, how often is one invited to join with like-minded individuals to partake in the eating of a human brain—let alone a famous brain?

Not, of course, *Einstein's* brain—that had turned up recently but, since it had been divided in very small pieces and distributed to scientists around the world, it wasn't likely to be featured as the main attraction for a dinner party. No, this was something very different.

The invitation was printed on hand-made rag paper—not ostentatiously thick—with simple, but (if you can forgive the expression) tasteful type. Garamond italic, I think—yes, I remember noticing that the lowercase "h" was almost closed, making the name of the featured entrée look like "Isbi's Brain," which only added to the confusion of the moment. But there it was:

*You are cordially invited
to participate in a singular dining experience,
featuring Sauté of Ishi's Brain
and a special libation created for the occasion.*

*Sunday, the 13th of September,
at the former estate of Douglas Fairbanks, Sr.*

RSVP

My first thought was that it was a prank.

I had published an account of the time when Fairbanks and Daisy Fellowes served an elegant meal of grilled human flesh to William Bueller Seabrook. It took place at a chateau near Paris, in 1932—after the publication of the book, *Jungle Ways*, in which Seabrook gave an account of his own cannibal experiences in West Africa.

The invitation seemed *too* perfect, too specifically attuned to my own rather *outré* tastes, to be true. However, so many people have asked me if I would ever try human flesh that I felt I was obliged to, at the very least, follow-up on the invitation. When I called to confirm, I discovered that the event was exactly as stated.

You remember who Ishi was? In 1911, in Oroville, California, a fifty-year-old Indian walked out of the hills—where he had been living in the Stone Age—and into a modern world that was incomprehensible to him. He was the last surviving member of his tribe, and had never acquired even the simplest trappings of modern society. Needless to say, he became the darling of anthropologists. He lived out the remaining five years of his life as a kind of living specimen—in a museum, in fact—constantly probed and prodded by all kinds of scientists, from anatomists to linguists. When he died, even his brain was preserved for future study. At the time, no one could have guessed that Ishi's final examination would be carried out by an assembly of gastronomes.

I had plenty of reasons to turn down the invitation. The idea—of eating the brain of this dead Indian was—rather like the practice of cannibalism itself: simultaneously disgusting and attractive.

Besides, like most Americans, I was a bit squeamish about eating organ meats—and, since the discovery of Kuru disease among the Foré of Papua, I had decided to avoid eating nerve tissue of *any* animal. Mad cow disease, wasting disease in deer and elk, scrapie in sheep—these were all good reasons to be prudent about certain kinds of culinary adventures. However, I deduced that California's Sierras were a long way from New Guinea, and Ishi was the last survivor of the Yahi—a tribe that had no history of eating human flesh—so there was probably not much risk.

My researches had told me that the brain was one of the most desirable portions of the body for ancient cannibals. Hearts were often eaten, for strength by warriors, and the buttocks—described as "the big meat," by some natives of Vanuatu—were eaten first by starving ship-wreck victims. However, among the remains of cannibal feasts, scorched skulls—used both as cooking pot and serving dish—indicate the popularity of the organ of reason as a culinary treat. The Fijians even made a special four-pronged wooden fork, the tines of which could be compressed to fit through the *foramen magnum* at the base of the skull—which allowed the fat-rich meat to be pulled through without affecting the collectability of the empty receptacle. Speaking of collectability, the gift shop of the Cannibal Museum, in Fiji, sells these forks to tourists. In fact, one of them stands—prongs upward—in a jar on my desk. It's just a conversation starter (or stopper—depending, naturally, on who's visiting my office), and I'm reasonably certain that it has never been used for its original intended purpose.

But I was telling you about what was going on in my *own* brain in response to the invitation. Weighing the risks of contracting some form of mind-destroying spongiform encephalopathy against the opportunity to experience a civilized version of an ancient culinary treat, I decided that I would be a fool not to attend the unusual *soirée*.

However, the risk of disease was not the only thing troubling me. There was the question of the preservation of Ishi's brain. It was, after all, essentially potted meat of a very rare and delicate type. I had to assume that formaldehyde was not used, or the "specimen"—or "main ingredient"—would have lost all culinary value in the ninety years or so that had passed since it was placed in its jar. What would be the point of eating something—no matter how rare—if it had lost its most significant culinary properties?

It would be like drinking a bottle of Haut-Brion from Thomas Jefferson's cellar, reduced by age to a vinegary sludge of ancient tannins and blackened pigment. Drinking such wine has little to do with taste, but much to do with conspicuous consumption. Better to leave some things in their bottles.

On the other hand, there would be only *one* chance to try this particular dish. Imagine having been given the chance to taste the last *suprême* of Passenger Pigeon—or *rôti* of Irish Elk or *entrecôte* of Mastodon. Wouldn't I forever regret the lost opportunity?

Then again, poor Ishi had been reduced to being a specimen, little more than an object for the curiosity of rich white men. Wasn't this just a more extreme version of that curiosity? Cannibals have often targeted the Other for dinner (or, alternatively, the charge of cannibalism has been used, by non-cannibals, to define the Other as somehow less human than civilized folk—which served as a wonderfully effective justification for colonial slavery or extermination of native peoples). Let's face it—the act of ingestion makes an object of another person. Was this something to which I wanted to be party? Could there be a more blatant example of the destruction of native America—by the descendants of white Europeans—than a formal dinner party at which the last remnant of an extinct tribe is served as the *pièce de résistance*?

Still, as Seabrook needed to fully understand "the precise thing that makes a cannibal a cannibal," so did I. If I were ever to be taken seriously as a student of cannibalism, wouldn't I *have* to attend this dinner?

So, after all the back-and-forth arguments, I decided that I *would* attend the dinner, After all, I could always decide—at the last minute—not to taste Ishi's last remains.

At the appointed hour, I arrived at the former Fairbanks estate—still uncertain, in my mind, about how, or *if*, I was to proceed, but determined to keep an open mind about the main event. I was also curious to see who else was invited.

The estate itself was ever-so-slightly run down, but the elegance of its former days was still evident—in its Old California architectural details, luxuriously mature gardens and liveried servants. I was led through a hall lined with Moorish tiles to a huge dining room—with a fireplace that covered most of the back wall, a black heavily-carved oaken table set with crystal and softly gleaming silver, and twelve arm-chairs, in the same carved oak, but with leather-covered seats.

Ten men were standing before the fireplace, chatting—I thought, 'though I might have been projecting a bit—a little nervously. I recognized a couple of writers, and was introduced to an odd mixture of anthropologists, historians, an artist, a sociologist, an explorer, and even an economist. If one of these men was our host, no one informed me of the fact. I *was* told that one more guest was expected—a newspaper advice columnist who attempted to answer readers' everyday ethical problems.

It amused me to imagine that such a columnist might still be struggling with the same concerns that had plagued me—if there was ever a list of ethical conundrums, this had to be near the top. Perhaps I was right, since—as it turned out—he never showed up. Perhaps the chance to taste such a rare dish was not enough—for him, unlike the rest of us—to outweigh the ethical conflicts occasioned by the invitation's arrival. Perhaps his failure to RSVP was a smaller ethical lapse that got lost among all the other philosophical complexities surrounding this event.

It *is* possible to overthink some situations—and this might well have been one of them.

The butler appeared—in that oddly silent manner that butlers have, a kind of shimmering emergence that suggests that butlers can spontaneously condense out of thin air, but wouldn't think of intruding until needed—and thanked us for coming. He suggested that, as some of us had traveled some distance, we might care for an *aperitif*—and he motioned us in the direction of a door to the adjoining library.

On another table, inside—much like the dining table already described, but quite a bit smaller—stood a dozen martini glasses and several silver cocktail shakers, their lightly-misted exteriors implying icy contents. The party moved—in erratic little jerks—towards the table, apparently torn between their conflicting desires to appear nonchalant while really, *really*, needing those drinks.

The butler, who had somehow managed to get to the table ahead of the thirsty mob, poured the needed libations. Someone suggested a toast to the host—whomever he or she might be—who had brought us all together that evening. We all looked around, but as no one admitted being the host, we simply toasted (so to speak) Ishi, and took our first gulp of our martinis.

Once past that first life-saving swallow, we sipped the rest of our drinks in a less impetuous manner. The cocktails were clearly not made with gin—their flavor suggested high-powered neutral spirits, somewhat vodka-like but softened slightly, and without the usual trace of vermouth. We looked at each other, quizzically, saw that no answer was immediately forthcoming, then turned to the butler.

He stood, silently of course, behind his table, with only the barest hint of an expression on his face—an expression, by the way, which none of us could have identified at the time. He said nothing until directly queried, at which point he took a deep breath, and answered.

"As you all know, this evening's meal will feature a rather rare—no, unique—dining experience. Your host, sensitive to the uncommon nature of tonight's ingredient, wanted to make sure that no portion was wasted. Additionally, as the anthropologist in your party can explain better than can I, some tribes of cannibals—endocannibals, yes?—believe that, in consuming the remains of their deceased relatives, some essence of the dearly departed is literally kept 'in the family.' It was decided, early in the planning of this evening's entertainment, to make use of every part of 'the guest of honor.' In place of vodka, tonight's spirit of preference is the pure ethyl alcohol in which Ishi's brain has marinated for nearly a century."

There was almost whistling "whoosh!" sound—in unintentional eleven-part harmony—as all the guests inhaled suddenly through nearly clenched teeth.

Some of the men started to set their glasses down, thought better of it, then tasted the drink again, in a more meditative manner. The explorer laughed, a little too heartily perhaps, and tossed back the remains of his cocktail. The sociologist *did* place his glass on the table—but it was nearly empty anyway. He merely watched as the others fiddled with their glasses, while exchanging the usual jokes about cannibalism. He noticed that I was watching *him*, and whispered that the others were beginning to form into two groups. It didn't surprise him that the academics stood together—but the fact that the explorer fit in with the artsy types struck him as unusual.

After a while, the butler returned to tell us that dinner was about to be served. We returned to the original room, where an appetizer course had been placed atop the elegant china. I was curious to see how our host approached the dinner, thematically.

The meal might feature rare and unusual dishes—such as ortolan or coelacanth—to respect the uniqueness of the main course. It could—'though I hoped it wouldn't—be designed to test our squeamishness thresholds, gradually building from one very creepy dish to another. I didn't want to believe that this entire meal might be little more than an upscale version of *Fear Factor*. Since the portion-size of the main course would be small (a one and a half pound brain would yield only two ounces, uncooked weight, per person), the meal might consist of a series of tiny courses, such as *tapas*, *dim sum* and *sushi*, the ultimate in *cuisine minceur*. Brain (at least the non-human one I'd tried before) does not have much in the way of flavor and texture—it's a richer, carnivore's, version of *tofu*—so I didn't expect the dishes preceding it to be so spicy or deeply-flavored that they would lessen the impact of the main course. The meal could be historically-based—in which case, it might reflect the dining habits of Californians in 1916, or possibly the foods that Ishi himself might have eaten. This last, while it had a certain Alice-Waters-eat-locally charm, was less appealing when one considers the fact that Ishi was starving when he risked leaving the Sierras to go to a place where—based on what he knew had happened to the rest of his people—he assumed he would be killed.

I hoped that the appetizer course would provide an answer to my thematic questions. The contents of the small plate did not, however, resolve much for me. It was a tiny hard-boiled quail's egg, topped with a few grains of *osetra* caviar. The appetizer was rare—but not exceedingly so (*osetra* is not even the highest quality of caviar—but it may have been chosen for its size, which was better proportioned to the quail egg). The ingredients *could* have been from California (but probably weren't). Ishi *could* have eaten quail eggs, but I doubted that he ever encountered sturgeon in the streams of the Sierras—and wealthy Californians *could* have served an appetizer like that, but I'd have to look that up to know for sure. The dish *was* tiny—but it was only an appetizer, after all. It was a relief to see that the *Fear Factor* approach was not in evidence.

The white-gloved servants cleared the appetizer plates, then the butler signaled for the soup tureen to be brought in. Into each tiny crystal bowl—which I thought unusual for soup—a ladleful of sparkling clear *Consommé de Perdreau* was poured, garnished with a tiny shaving of white truffle in the form of an arrowhead. The shape—clearly meant as an allusion to Ishi's skills as a flint-napper—was a little too obviously camp for my taste, but the Tuscan truffle imparted a delicate but sensuous perfume to the soup that was, itself, marvelously subtle, with delicate color, absolute clarity and a decadently rich mouth-feel.

I was so taken with the soup that it took me a while to remember that I was looking for evidence of a thematic pattern. The soup was composed of rare, but not ridiculously rare, ingredients—certainly not local ones, at least. It might have been part of an elegant meal in the teens of the last century, but we can be certain that Ishi never savored anything like it. I was reassured that, once again, there was nothing about the soup course that might generate feelings of disgust in any of us.

After the soup plates and bouillon spoons were removed—and a fish fork added to the elegant cutlery at each place setting—the butler poured the first wine, a Schramsberg *Blanc de Blancs* from Calistoga. Servers, in pairs, then pooled reduced cream and sliced morels onto our plates, topped by a poached fillet of wild golden trout. A deep green sprig of watercress rested beside the pink fillet, its mildly peppery crunch playing against the unctuous combination of fish, cream and wild mushrooms. This was the first substantial course of the meal, effectively eliminated the *cuisine minceur* theme. All the ingredients were relatively local, though fairly rare. Golden trout, found only in the icy streams of the Sierra Nevadas, are wild—not farm-raised like those bland and soft-textured rainbows found in grocery stores and mediocre restaurants—and can only be had, legally, by those willing to fish for them. The meal might have been served, historically, and Ishi would have had access to all its components, except for the cream. Only a determined fish- (or mushroom-) hater could have found anything objectionable in that course.

Once again, the plates and used silver were removed, and again the butler poured the new wine. I was expecting, as the meat course was next, a red—perhaps, considering the delicate nature of the meat, a lighter red; a pinot noir or, possibly, one of the lighter zinfandels—but I was mistaken. The choice this time was another Schramsberg sparkler—*Cuvée de Pinot*—a delicate pink wine with a little more body than the *Blanc de Blancs*, and only the slightest hint of fruit.

At a nod from the butler, plated entrées were placed before each of us at the table. In unison, the servers took a step back, and stood behind each chair.

Fanned out, like the rays of the setting sun (or, as one the guests quipped, a war bonnet's feathers) were leaves of Belgian endive. At the base of each leaf, a small dollop of Sauce Romesco sat atop a thin slice of Meyer lemon. These glowing dots peeked out from behind a cloud-shaped half-inch-thick transverse slice of buttery golden-brown brain. The two lobes were clearly visible, as were the distinctive furrows. Nothing about this dish was intended to hide its essential nature.

No one moved.

No one spoke (even the wise guy who had made the war bonnet comment was silent).

I don't know what others were doing then, there was only the plate before me. I cut off a tiny piece from the edge—thinking, "this is the gray matter; this is the part that held Ishi's conscious thoughts; this is the part that separates humans from the lower animals; this is *us*."

It was a little firmer than I expected. Usually brains are poached in *court bouillon*, to firm them, so they can be sliced for the final cooking—but this required no preparatory firming. I wondered, if like other muscles, the brain gets tougher and more flavorful through repeated use—then realized that, much as we don't like to admit it, animals have to use their brains too (even if we use them for different purposes).

Suddenly, the reason for the brain's texture was obvious: it was pickled! Ninety years in two-hundred proof alcohol had denatured the protein—and, no doubt, lowered its water content—creating a firm cheese-like texture.

I sniffed the bit on my fork: there were no unseemly aromas—certainly no formaldehyde—a trifle winy (no doubt from the pickling), but the primary scent was of browned meat and butter.

I put it in my mouth.

The first taste sensation was that of warm butter, followed by a little saltiness, some pepper, the savoriness of browned meat. I chewed. It was slightly crispy on the outside, and chewy on the inside—rather like cheap over-cooked veal cutlets, but without their fibrous quality. The browned outside reinforced the veal cutlet impression, but the smoothness of the interior reminded me more of low-fat mozzarella; it almost squeaked a little when I bit into it.

I dipped the second piece in some of Romesco. I hadn't wanted anything to disguise the taste of the meat at first, but now wanted to see if there was any reason for choosing the sauce—beyond its nod to California's Spanish heritage. It was a big improvement. Typically served with grilled chicken or fish, the garlicky red pepper, tomato and almond paste worked beautifully with the fat buttery taste of the meat. Likewise, the bitter endive leaves worked a kind of culinary counterpoint against the roundness of the other flavors. A sip of the Schramsberg cleared the palate, so that I could go back and taste everything anew.

I looked up, and saw that everyone else was eating—some pensively, some hurriedly—but no one was gagging, no one had pushed away from the table, no one was gulping wine defensively. I finished eating everything on my plate, and sat back in my heavy oaken chair, to digest—both the meal and the experience.

There was a salad course and dessert, but I don't remember anything noteworthy about them.

I recalled my earlier determination to discover an underlying pattern in the meal's structure. I noted that the main course *was* unusual (indeed, it would be hard to imagine a less common main ingredient). It *was* small and somewhat precious in its presentation, as befitted its rarity. It *was* certainly local and historical in its ingredients and allusions. What amazed me was the complete lack of *Fear Factor* responses it *could* have generated, but didn't.

Of course, we were *way* past that once the butler served his surprise cocktails at the beginning of the evening—but the real reason I had experienced no wave of revulsion was the discovery that Ishi's brain was just meat. There was nothing especially noteworthy about it, beyond what was done with it in the kitchen—just like everything else on the menu.

RECIPES

Daube de Duke of Clarence
When you are ready to dispatch your duke, be sure to limp about and rave incongruously, and maybe call for a horse. Place him to marinate in a butt of malmsey and aromatics for about a week. Then stew your duke with cinnamon, cloves, onions and some verjuice. Serve on bread trenchers or in bowls on sops. Garnish with some currants and blanched almonds. This must be eaten with your fingers.

Ken Albala

Ol' Fashioned St. Lawrence Barbecue
First find a Third Century Saint noted for his pious donations to the poor. Prepare a hot bed of coals under a sturdy grill. Lash your saint to the grill and barbecue, waiting for instructions from him when to be turned over. He should be well cooked to remove the flavor of sanctity. When fully cooked and crisp serve him with a good smoky barbecue sauce.

Ken Albala

Kofteh "Fille du Pape" Chez Voltaire
First obtain a delectable young girl who claims to be the daughter of Pope Urban X. Next don a turban and brandish a fearsome scimitar and pretend than you are under siege by the Russians. In desperation, eat a few eunuchs. Then turn to the girl. Carefully slice off a single buttock cheek and finely mince. Mix this with soaked bulghur wheat, garlic, cumin and mint, and form into thighs or any other body part that seems appropriate. Fry and serve hot with yoghurt sauce, judiciously drizzled.

Ken Albala

Donner Party Mix
First find an obscenely cold place and fill it with as much snow as you can manage. Invite some friends over. Have everyone

disrobe down to their undies for dramatic effect. When someone dies, carefully remove the frostbitten parts and cut the skin and subcutaneous fat into strips. Deep fry these and season with salt, chili powder, and onion powder. Start the party. Alternatively, reserve part of the skin, inflate, and play football in the snow.

Ken Albala

Rockefeller Mountain Oysters

When you really want to impress someone, at an intimate dinner for two, there's no substitute for rich foods made from rare and expensive ingredients. This most delicate of meats should be served as an upscale *amuse-gueule* with a cool (not chilled) White Graves, preferably a youngish Laville Haut-Brion.

Separate the oysters from unusable portions of the Rockefeller (which can, if cost is an issue, be reserved for another purpose, such as the next), trimming carefully to reveal two exquisite jewels. Place half oyster shells (preferably ones with a lustrous lining of nacre) in a thick layer of rock salt, in an ovenproof serving dish. Prepare a bed of coarsely chopped watercress in each pearly shell.

Lay the opulent orbs gently amid the greens, top with seasoned butter and fine crumbs of brioche.

Roast in preheated broiler, until a soft popping sound signals that dinner, and the end of a dynasty, is at hand.

Serves 2.

Gary Allen

Rockefeller Rockefeller (as an *al fresco* entrée)

Take one human. Roast over open fire pit.

Lay on bed of sea salt, made from evaporated seawater.

Cut up 2 to 5 pounds of sago, depending on size of human and taste.

Heat sago over fire. Beat into mushy consistency with pointed sticks (axeheads as available). Smoke many tobacco pipes while waiting for human, then sago, to cook.

Season human with sago to taste.

Serves 24.

Gene Santoro

Bush Almondine

Here's a down-home recipe I like better than 'possum or 'gator. Texas Bush is the best to use for this recipe, but Florida Bush will work if you boil the meat before you bake it.

2 Cups	Bleached Rice, cooked
3 Cups	Baked Bush, diced
2	10 3/4 oz. cans, condensed Cream of Mushroom soup
1/2 Cup	Real mayonnaise
1/3 Cup	Cheney brains (use squirrel if needed), grated
1 Tbsp.	Canned Rove
1 Tbsp.	Salt
2 1/4 Cups	Corn flakes, crushed
3 oz.	Almonds, sliced

Mix together and place in thin baking dish. Bake at 350 degrees for 30 minutes.

M.L. McCorkle

SOMETHING FROM THE OVEN

"...while I was being chewed by her I felt also that I was acting on her, transmitting sensations that spread from the taste buds though her whole body. I was the one who aroused her every vibration—it was a reciprocal and complete relationship, which involved and overwhelmed us."
(Italo Calvino, *Under the Jaguar Sun*)

UNDERTAKER: Can I have a look? She looks quite young.
MAN: Yes, yes, she was.
UNDERTAKER: *(calling):* Fred!
FRED'S VOICE: Yeah?
UNDERTAKER: I think we've got an eater.
MAN: What?!?
FRED: *(peeking head round the door)*
Right, I'll get the oven on. *(goes off)*
MAN: Er, excuse me, um... are you suggesting eating my mother?
UNDERTAKER: Er... yeah, not raw. Cooked.
MAN: What?
UNDERTAKER: Yes, roasted with a few french fries, broccoli, horseradish sauce...
MAN: Well, I do feel a bit peckish.
UNDERTAKER: Great!
MAN: Can we have some parsnips?
UNDERTAKER: *(calling):* Fred... get some parsnips.
MAN: I really don't think I should.
UNDERTAKER: Look, tell you what... we'll eat her, if you feel a bit guilty about it after, we can dig a grave and you can throw up in it.
(Monty Python)

LAST REQUEST
Dennis DiClaudio

Donald made it perfectly clear that when he died he wanted us, his friends, to eat him. "Do this one thing for me," he said in the living room of his apartment. Buddhist monks have been doing this sort of thing for years in China. He said this would allow him to live on through us. His flesh could nourish our bodies, and we would carry him into an old age he himself would never live to see. He walked onto the balcony with his beer and stared out at the city lights. Our initial reaction was mixed. It was a lot to take in. First our friend was dying, and now he wanted us to eat him. We didn't know what to think. It was grotesque. And possibly dangerous. On the other hand, we were his only family—both his parents had died when he was a child; he had no brothers or sisters—and, it was his last request after all. How could we deny him that? So, after some deliberation, we decided that yes, we would eat Donald.

He had a tumor. A malignant growth pushing itself across the two hemisphere's of his brain. That was lucky for us, because we figured there'd be little desiccation of the meat the way there'd be if he had a disease, like hantavirus pulmonary syndrome. He was a pretty big guy—a football player in college—so, if everything worked out okay, there'd be plenty of meat for all of us. Tony went home and scoured the internet, researching the safest way to cook human flesh, to insure that it's not harmful. The rest of us went through our cookbooks, looking for the best, most fitting way, to prepare our good friend.

A few weeks later, while I was playing soccer in the park, Margot called me. "Donald's having spells of dizziness," she said. "He's checked himself into the hospital." I excused myself from the game and went to be by Donald's side. When I arrived in the waiting room, nearly everyone else was there already. Patrick and Keenan were off in a corner, in heated discussion, and Margot was at the reception desk, trying to get information on Donald's condition. It was Patrick's opinion that human flesh should taste like pork, since we have roughly the same size, weight and diet as a pig. Keenan disagreed, saying he'd read, in the biography of an escaped gulag prisoner who'd been forced to eat his companion, that human flesh tastes like a light beef and that we'd be well off to consider recipes tailored toward veal.

No sooner did Margot discover that Donald was definitely considered a lost cause than Tony arrived, carrying a print-out from an anthropology website that claimed human meat will not prove harmful so long as it is cooked well. This annoyed Keenan, who was hoping for a dish prepared with a slight braise. He said that he guessed he could throw out the recipe for lemongrass veal salad he'd found. Margot told him to shut up and be happy that he was getting anything at all. I was concerned about contracting some form of spongiform encephalopathy, but Tony assured us that those things only occur in cases of habitual cannibalism. We should be fine, he said, so long as we didn't acquire a taste. Margot did not laugh.

When we were finally allowed to see Donald, he was lying on a bed with tubes coming out of his arms and spiraling into machines that made rhythmic beeping sounds. He was drugged and barely recognized us. He opened his eyes as thin crescents and smiled weakly. Patrick voiced some concern that the drugs might alter Donald's taste. "I think they might make him bitter," he said. Margot glowered, but it was a genuine concern. I offered to speak with the doctor and see if our friend couldn't be keep kept as pain-free as possible, but without too much damage the final product. Just after we were ushered out, I pulled a nurse aside, and she said she'd do what she could.

The next day, Donald was much more lucid, talking with us and even laughing occasionally. But, he had a hollow look about him. Death was no longer an abstract concept, as it had been when he'd first told us about the tumor. It was a real thing that was coming. He held my hand. Tears welled in his eyes. Margot recalled something she'd read in a book about Buddhism, something about being illusory. She explained it as watching a garter snake slither past a slit in a fence. "It's all one snake," she said, "even if we can only see the tail. The head is still out there somewhere." He nodded in agreement, but I'm not certain he understood her point. It didn't seem to make either of them feel any better. Margot bit down on her lip and looked to the white tile floor.

Keenan, when he arrived, was carrying a book under his arm, *Fifty One Savory Veal Dishes*, for which Margot and Tony scolded him as being in very bad taste. I have to say that I agreed. He apologized to Donald, which kind of just made matters worse. "I just came from the book store," he said. "I didn't want to make an extra trip home." Donald shrugged his shoulders and said that it was okay, but his eyes kept darting back to the book, which Keenan had placed on the chair with our coats. Patrick was also a bit miffed and at some point blurted out, rather non-sequentially, "So, we've decided on veal, have we?" I assured Patrick that we had not decided on anything yet and told him to just relax. Keenan made an exasperated face and mumbled, under his breath, "Twenty-three dollars down the tube," but we all heard him. Donald looked a bit green, and then a nurse came in and shooed us all away, saying he needed rest. It was decided that all further discussions of preparation would be kept to the waiting room area.

What none of us had realized was just how long it can take for a person to die. Weeks passed. Donald lay in his bed watching soap operas, flipping through travel magazines. Meanwhile, we tacked recipes to our refrigerators and watched helplessly as our friend shed pound after pound. He stopped eating. The specter of death was ruining his appetite. We snuck him hamburgers and milkshakes under our coats, but the food went untouched. He had no appetite. He looked up at us and asked if we thought he'd led a good life. This was all very distressing. "Marbling is the key," Patrick reminded us. "Without the fat, it might as well all be flank." We nodded in silent agreement. I, for one, had been hoping for some nice tender medallions to sauté in a saltimbocca sauce. Tony showed us charts that outlined the way a person could be cut up for cooking purposes and said, gravely, that he thought he could still manage some decent cuts regardless. This made us all feel a little better, except for Margot who said she was having second thoughts. Keenan brought her outside to talk. Through the window, I watched them share a cigarette, silhouetted against the light from a street lamp. When they returned, Margot agreed to make good on her promise after all. She has a professional quality kitchen and a fantastic collection of wines, so her involvement was highly desired.

As Donald's condition continued to deteriorate, we spent more and more time at his bedside and eventually began taking turns spending the night with him. I was in and out of sleep in a chair one night, using my jacket as a blanket. Margot had brought a portable CD player into the room. She and Donald stayed up late, without talking, listening to old Blue Note disks. I remember waking with The Miles Davis Quartet coming softly from the floor to my left. Donald, half the size that he'd been when he'd made his request over drinks, was staring blankly toward the ceiling. Margot was tracing shapes in his bed sheets with her finger. Without looking away from the ceiling, Donald whispered, "Margot, I want you to have my Steely Dan records." Margot started crying and ran out into the hall. Donald looked to me, his shoulders hunched in exhaustion and said, "I can't go on like this."

Keenan called me a few days later with some interesting news. "Tony's dead." "You mean Donald," I said. "No," he said, "Tony." Somewhere between his office and the hospital, Tony had been run down by a motor scooter. It was a terrible shock for all of us—except for Donald, who at that point was under heavy sedation. Keenan, Patrick and I went outside to smoke a cigarette. None of us spoke, but we were all thinking the same thing. Finally, Patrick broke the silence. "I've been considering it, and it's now my opinion that human meat might taste like goat." He'd found a fabulous curry recipe, he said. Keenan nodded his head gravely and said, "Maybe... maybe... " Reluctantly, we concluded that Tony had never led us to believe that his last wishes were in any way similar to Donald's. Patrick looked a little deflated, but he shrugged off the disappointment. "Tony's too skinny anyway," he said, and we nodding in solemn agreement. When we got back to Donald's room, Margot was at his bedside, her face nestled into his palm. We quietly backed our way out of the room and went across the street for a drink.

That night, I was woken up by a phone call. It was Margot. Her voice was deep with emotion. "You know," she said, "he could be very tender when he wanted to be." I was half-asleep and confused. I wasn't sure if the call was a dream. "What?" I said. Then she told me. Donald had died only fifteen minutes earlier. I heard the phone slip from her hand and onto the floor.

Everybody mourns differently. Some drape themselves in black. Others beat their breasts and rend their clothes. We mourned our friend by marinating an excellent cut of tenderloin in a sweet and sour sauce made with fresh apricots and then broiling it until it was just a hair below medium well and serving it on a bed of steamed asparagus beside roasted potatoes rubbed with garlic and a buttery French cabernet that Patrick had been saving for a special occasion. The table seemed empty without Donald's presence. (Oddly, Tony was barely mentioned.) Before we ate, Keenan proposed a toast. "To a dear friend who will be very sadly missed." We raised our glasses and tapped them together. The room filled briefly with the tinkling music of our tribute. I watched Margot down her wine, place the glass on the table and bring a forkful of the tenderloin to her mouth. I watched as she pursed her lips around the fork and withdrew it empty. The angular outline of her jaw working beneath a flushed undulating cheek as she slowly, thoughtfully masticated the carefully prepared cuisine. I watched her close her eyes, lift her chin slightly and swallow. Only then did I begin to eat.

THE ECHO

Richard O'Corozine

AN EXCERPT FROM A ONE-ACT PLAY

Characters: **Peter**, a middle-aged man. Stocky, dark; wears glasses, dark overcoat, suit underneath, black laceless shoes.
The Boy, aged 17-18. Fair-haired; wears glasses, dark suit, black laceless shoes.
Mother, well-kept, 60-70 years old, wears glasses, black dress. Stocky build.

Scene I: An empty lot in a wind-storm; the wind sound is audible. The "lot" is a raised area on the stage. On the perimeter is a "barricade" of wooden planks resting on boxes. At the center of the "lot" sits a small desk with a wooden chair. On the desk is a globe (to the left) and a TV monitor (to the right); to the right of the desk is a metal barrel with a simulated fire in it. On the barrel rests a grill with a frying pan. The light is golden dusk slowly darkening to night at the end of Scene I. In front of the raised area is a single chair.

Mother: Oh yes, yes, where was I? ...Around nine or so Mr. Testa called and told me my son did not show up nor call, and he was just calling to find out if everything was alright. I lied. I told Mr. Testa that he wasn't feeling well and that I had forgotten to call. I was frightened ...he had never done anything like this before ...missing school ...not calling ...I was scared that something was wrong ...the way he was that morning ...his sadness at seeing Mr. Testa leaving the school ...(pause, adjusts herself) ...I knew he had tutoring and there was one student who was having a particularly difficult time, who he was helping. This boy was difficult. In trouble a lot. Cutting classes, trouble with the other students. My son wanted to help him, that's all, that's what he wanted to do. The boy was difficult, drugs, alcohol, I don't know what, I don't know the difference, but he was *so* difficult that my son ...good-hearted that he was ...wanted to help him. He met with the boy every day. I never thought that he felt ...(pauses, adjusts herself) ...oh, I don't know ...What was it? Did he think of his father? Was he trying to get back at his father? Or me? ...Me? Good Jesus, I raised him ...the mother, the poor mother ...poor, poor mother ...what she has to endure for her child. What I've had to endure since that day ...(pause) ...I was frantic and felt that something terrible had happened. A mother's intuition I guess. I wanted to call the police, but about what: My son didn't go to school! They would laugh at me, and worse, contact Mr. Testa ...and what would he think? He'd know that my son lied and ...my son ...(pause) Well, I'm sure Mr. Testa now knows the story about him, and how I lied to cover for my son. I mean I had to protect him. I always have haven't I? And I always will! ...(pause) When he was thirteen ...I've always kept this in the back of my mind ...I thought it was just the idle ramblings of a juvenile, the unpleasant nightmares of a young boy nearing manhood ...he had a particular disposition and now that I look back I think it meant more than I imagined. ...Well, I waited for him to come home. I just sat on the couch and stared at the TV. It was off, I remember, and I was too frightened to go over and turn it on. The phone didn't ring, no one came to the door, it was as if he had been swallowed up on that day. Finally, sometime around five I heard a car in the driveway, I ran to the door and out into the yard and there he was walking up the sidewalk... "I got held up at school today," he said as he walked past me and into the house ...He *lied!* ...He lied to me! I mean he had never lied to me, and here I knew he lied. I didn't know what to do, what to say to him.

So, I went into the house and asked all the normal questions: How was school? How is Mr. Testa? How was the tutoring? Is the young boy, Pete, coming for extra help this evening? He answered me in a low voice with no enthusiasm: "Fine, mother, fine ...Yes mother ...I think he will be over tonight." With that he went to the kitchen. I was confused. He seemed fine, but he had lied to me and he acted as if nothing was wrong. Like he had a normal day, a day at school, like all the hundreds of others ...talking to the students, talking with Mr. Testa. I decided to call Mr. Testa, perhaps he was late to school and had shown up after Mr. Test called, and then he simply forgot to call me back. Mr. Testa answered the phone and immediately inquired as to my son's health ..."Fine, fine" I said. "he should be in tomorrow Mr. Testa." ...He lied to me! He lied to me! He hadn't gone to work! Where was he all day? Why did he lie to me? He had never lied before ...never! I taught him to always be truthful ...always! I was so worried ...(pause, shaking her head) ...He went to his room and locked the door. I knocked but he wouldn't answer, and I remembered when he was thirteen. I remember it like yesterday. He had come to me in the morning. He had wakened strangely ...from one of those deep sleeps that I mentioned ...those that absolutely terrify me ...and tried to tell me about the dreams he had been having that were terrifying him. Recurring dreams. Dreams of horror, of horrible things that he did ...to, to other people ...disgusting things! I couldn't listen to it, I told him to shut up, and I slapped him across the face ...I slapped him to make him stop, to make him stop telling me, to make him stop the dreams ...He just looked at me ...a look I had never seen before, and then just smiled and walked away. He went to his room and locked the door. After a few minutes I knocked on his door but he didn't answer. I tried to open it but it was locked. I called to him and banged on the door with my hands, but still there was no answer. I was worried, that look on his face, self-assured and cruel, a look that knew something that I didn't and it scared me. I tried to coax him out and I remembered those days when he had stayed home because the children at school had laughed ...(pause, adjusting herself) ...He didn't answer. His room was quiet, *too* quiet, you know what I mean? Too quiet, like there was no life in there, like it was empty ...but I knew he was in there, I knew it ...it's just ...(shaking her head) ...it was *too quiet*! I tried everything to get him out, but there was no answer, no sound at all. I thought of him in that deep sleep and it frightened me. I ran to the kitchen and called Father Cullen, the priest at our church. I told him what was happening and he remembered the ripped pants episode without me mentioning it, saying: "Yes. Yes, he has a very fragile disposition, perhaps the Lord can calm his mind ...offer him love." I asked him to come over and talk to him, to "offer him love" ...Good Jesus I certainly had! Father said he would come ...(pause) ...I went back to his door and knocked...

Peter: (he stops walking) Yes ...(he said quietly)

Mother: Open the door, I must see you.

Peter: Yes, yes...

Mother: (screamed) *Open the door!*

Peter: How? How do I do it? (walking the perimeter)

Mother: (scared) Do what?

Peter: Do I open it?

Mother: Yes, yes, of course you open it, of course you do...

Peter: Yes, yes ...(stops walking) ...there is no door.

Mother: Of course there is, open it ...*open it!*

Peter: (continues walking) Of course there is ...yes, yes, of course there is ...yes, yes ...

Mother: ...He was mimicking me. Mimicking me ...that was not my son behind that door ...my son never mimicked anyone, least of all his mother, the person he loved most ...I knocked again...

Peter: (stops walking) Yes ...yes, yes.

Mother: ...My heart was in my throat. I felt as if I was losing the only thing I ever loved. It was like I could *feel* him slipping far, far away. I kept knocking and finally I heard him near the door, turning the knob, trying to open it. I pushed it open as he unlocked it, and he stepped back as I came into his room and stared at me ...his eyes open wide like he had never seen me before. He looked alright, but he didn't seem to recognize me. I called his name but he just stood there, looking through me ...and then, you know, he did the strangest thing. *He took a candy from his pocket ...like a little red ball, like those that his father had given him when he was a baby ...and popped it into his mouth. His whole concentration was on that candy, and he held up the cellophane wrapper and let it drop to the floor (PETER acts out this sequence)*...the look on his face ...I mean he was smiling, but in a puzzled way, like he didn't know the source of his pleasure ...He slowly started to walk around the room, around the walls, not in the middle of the room, but near the walls ...and he took those little steps ...(pause, adjusts herself) ...A nightmare, Father Cullen said ...he had just woken from one of those twilight dreams that seem more real than real, and that take forever to come out from ...I've never forgotten the expression on my son's face: empty, filled with pleasure, but empty of life. Father Cullen had come to talk to him, but by then he had woken up and had no memory of the episode. Father told me to relax, but to see a doctor ...that maybe something was wrong with his nervous system, or his brain was maybe not getting the right mix of blood and oxygen, or maybe, just maybe, it was a one-time thing …only happen once …I prayed, it was better after talking to Father, and my son felt better. Those horrible nightmares (shaking her head) …horrible, horrible. No wonder he would wake up in a trance, he was scared to death, he was, scared to death …(adjusts herself) …So, this time, I knocked and called to him, but let him be. I was worried, but not like that time, when he was thirteen, that was the last time he ever did that! You know, that trance that he was in, and he was alright …wasn't he? He was alright! …(pauses, adjusts her clothes) The next thing I remember was the sound of voices, loud voices, that woke me up. I got out of bed. I was frightened, the voices seemed to be coming from all over the house. I called to my son, but there was no answer. The voices continued, but they were not my son. A few voices, but none of them my son's. I called to him again, but no answer. No one could hear me. I looked at the clock and it was around one A.M. …late it was. My son and I are usually fast asleep by eleven …What were the voices? Who were they? …A radio? …No, no, no …I wanted to go to the living room, the phone is there, and I wanted to call the police. Through the window there was a flashing red light …it *was* the police! What were they doing here? I ran to my door but it was locked, from the outside. Locked! Who could have locked me in but my son …he knew the police would come …he knew how embarrassed I would be to know what he had done …he knew, yes, yes, he knew …Finally the police opened my door, they told me there had been an accident earlier in the day and that they wanted to talk to my son… "What kind of accident?" I asked them, but they didn't answer …They said they had to take my son to the station and that I could go in another car if I wished …I kept asking about the accident, but they wouldn't answer ...I went with them to the station, I didn't know a thing ...I still don't understand ...(she pause, adjusts her clothes) ...I don't understand. I mean, how could he do such a thing? Something like that! Like they say ...(she crosses herself and adjusts her clothes) ...He was always such a good boy, such a good boy ...He *is* a good boy, still, a good boy, yes, yes ...teacher of the year, how many can say that? ...everybody loved him, everybody! ...he was so well liked, so well ...yes, yes ...Good Jesus, how did this happen? (crosses herself again) ...I raised him to be nice, to be polite, a nice boy, kind, caring. A good boy, nice to people ...helping others to do whatever, anything, just to be nice ...be nice ...and then he goes and does something like this, like they say he did ...How could he? *No, no,* no, no, no, no ..., *no*! It's impossible ...Good Jesus! Good Jesus help me! ...How can I show my face? Where do *I* go? Can they put me away too? Good Jesus, the embarrassment! How could he do this? Such a thing, how could he? (she crosses herself and begins to recite The Act of Contrition) ...Oh my God I am heartily sorry for having offended thee ...(she prays and her voice trails off ...she finished, crosses herself, then looks out at the audience) ...They took me down to the police station that night, they wanted to ask me questions. Yes, yes, they wanted to question me as to the where-abouts of my son ...they knew he wasn't in school, they had talked to Mr. Testa, and he had told them that I knew his where-abouts. I told them the truth, I didn't lie to them. They asked me about my son's friends, his relationships, if he had a woman friend, or anyone, that he was close to. "Only me," I told them, "only me." They smiled, but said little. I kept asking them if he was alright, was the accident serious. They said he was alright, but there was someone else involved, and it was serious. Another woman came into the station, much younger than myself, about my son's age, very attractive, tall, blond. They took her to another room and closed the door. In what seemed like seconds she was screaming, sobbing, shouting at the top of her lungs: "*Oh my God! Oh my God! ...Noooooooooooo ...Nooooooo ... No. No no no no no no ...*" I felt uncomfortable ...not only in embarrassment for her, for her lament, but I was connected to her, I could feel it. It was three in the morning and I still had no idea if and when I could see my son ...I was alone in the room, that room at the station, when I knew, the other woman's screams echoing through the building, and I knew. I just did. Mother's intuition I guess, but I did ...I knew ...I didn't know how, or why, or what, but I knew "who" ...my son had done something, there was no accident, he was responsible for that poor woman's lament ...But what? A fight? Maybe with this woman's husband? Maybe he had tried to help someone that she knew, maybe ...(pause) ...I had no idea that this woman was ...(pause) ...(choked up) The officer came into the room, a Detective it was, a Detective Nelson ...He looked at me and asked if I needed anything. "My son," I said. He stared at me, smiled, and took my hand ...He told me what happened ...Good Jesus, I was horrified. "My son! My son! ...Good Jesus, that's not possible," I told him. He said it happened as he said. I couldn't believe it, couldn't believe it ...my son ...my son ...a murderer ...a killer ...killed that boy ...his student ...the one he tried to help, Pete, yes, yes ...he killed him ...Good Jesus, how horrible The poor screaming woman? *His* mother ...in shock she was ...he killed that boy? ...every Wednesday night he was ...he killed Pete? ...Good Jesus, why? How could it be my boy ...It wasn't until later, days maybe, that I heard the details ...how they found that boy, and what my son had done to him ...that poor boy, and his poor, poor mother ...it was so embarrassing, so embarrassing ...(she stops, staring at the audience. She takes the compact from her purse and straightens her glasses, powders her nose, and runs a comb through her hair. She puts the compact back, adjusts her dress, and look back at the audience) ...Is there anything else? ...(pause) ...I would like to go, this has been a terrible ordeal for me ...(she exits—stage right) (PETER walks in circles around the perimeter of the lot as THE BOY follows on hands and knees. The scene fades to black)

Scene II: The lot, again. A solitary light hangs over the desk. The TV monitor is *on*, MOTHER's image silently re-telling the story. Her face is in extreme close-up. There is no wind, the stage is quiet (1 minute). Then, there is a scream (THE BOY), then silence again (30 seconds). From the darkness at the back of the stage walks PETER, as a small spot illuminates THE BOY, half in shadows, lying on his back, his pants pulled down and covered with blood. PETER walks to mid-stage; to the barrel with the grill and fry pan on it; his hands, covered in blood, are cupped and carrying something. He places it gently in the fry pan, and it sizzles (highly audible). He cooks it, poking at it with his fingers (the sound of the "food" cooking gets louder and louder—a sizzling, crackling sound, like bacon being cooked—*sound crescendo: 1 minute*)

Mother: (on TV—barely audible at first, then slowly moving throughout to highest possible volume) ... I still don't understand ...(she pause, adjusts her clothes) ...I don't understand. I mean, how could he do such a thing? Something like that! Like they say ...(she crosses herself and adjusts her clothes)

138

RIBS
Suzanne Rindell

Don was utterly fascinated by my zipper. It was one of those trendy zippers you saw a lot of nowadays, turning up on an increasing number of shirts and sweaters, the kind that had two runners and zipped both ways. When he asked if he could operate it I nodded and chattered on indifferently, picking at my salad with a black plastic fork and ignoring the pair of hands floundering at my chest. I watched as his hands worked it: three inches up, three inches down; top zipper up, bottom zipper down. And of course, everything tucked in neatly at all times of operation, as expected. But that's the way friendship works, I suppose. Friendship allows you to sit in Wendy's eating your Biggie Size Chinese Chicken Salad in complete confidence that the man tinkering with your zipper will make sure that no matter where his inspection leads him, all will stay in place and you don't have to worry about your sweater suddenly flying open and your braless breasts popping out for all the fast-food lunchtime population at Wendy's in Prairie City, Illinois to see. I peered into Don's face, watching his eyes squint and narrow. He had a very smooth forehead, I noticed, even when his brow was furrowed in concentration. Abruptly, Don concluded his investigation, all the while the thought of my braless breasts probably having never crossed his mind. Clothes won't have zippers at all in the future, he said, turning back to his Biggie Burger and Biggie Fries, his face bent down over the yellow crinkly paper wrapper. Their shape will be more continuous, more fitted to conform to the human body, more comfortable overall and more dependent upon Lycra in their thread content. More like the stretchy uniforms on Star Trek, he said. Don was a big fan of Star Trek. He knew all the episodes by their script numbers. Before I met Don, I'd only even seen one Star Trek episode in my entire life (Episode Number Forty-Two: *The Trouble with Tribbles*—but fortunately a very important one to know in Don's book). You don't realize how important a common metaphorical language is between two friends. But it is. I had a lot of catching up to do before I could thoroughly grasp the gist of Don's metaphors. I never told him that though. After our initial conversation in the elevator (during which I was able to directly quote one of Mr. Spock's lines of acumen from the whole *Tribbles* fiasco) Don took it as a sign of our "inherent" synergy and was pretty content to do most of the talking (or grunting, as the case may be) from there on out. This is not to say that Don was a talkative person in the slightest. No, he was decidedly not a talker. In fact, most of the time we spent together involved very little talking at all. But we ate a lot of lunches together, albeit most of them in silence.

Why were we friends, then? I suppose most people would assume it was because we worked at the same place and did similar research, though Don's research department was a great deal smaller (in total, it consisted of Don and one other man with the unlikely name of Bellalou). It was also much less marketable, from a company-and-consumer point of view. In the morning Don sat in a cubicle with the rest of us and ran data from experiments he'd performed the day before. But in the afternoons he disappeared. Don spent his afternoons in a very drippy, dank, dim little lab, doing research on starfish and particularly on the regenerative enzymes they produced when you cut off one of their arms and they had to re-grow it. There was no specific directive behind Don's research, no mission statement to speak of, and Don's research was very rarely included as a tiny blurb in the institute's brochures, if at all. But still, regenerative enzymes were regenerative enzymes, and if Don and Bellalou could find a way to manipulate and use them for some sort of human purpose, the institute's directors figured they would consequently find a way to market the whole operation in the end. My research was of a very different kind. Unlike Don's research, my work was fated to fall very directly into a large market of consumers' greedy little outstretched hands. I worked in the Cosmetic/Rejuvenation department, along with about 350 other researchers. The institute was quite large—about 900 people strong at any given time—but my department, the Cosmetic/Rejuvenation department, was one of the largest and most lucrative in the entire company. This was no small statement, as the institute generated several billion dollars a year. The founders kept a low profile, and the institute was touted as "an explorers' organization passionately committed to scientific discovery"—but the truth was, the institute was also a profit-generating company whose year-end figures easily qualified it to rank modestly among the *Fortune* 500. Financially speaking, we were bigger than some the nation's major pharmaceutical corporations.

Perhaps in part because of the town's blue-collar provincial aura, and perhaps in part because of the institute's looming size, we often fell into the habit of regarding ourselves as an island of civility, fatally stranded in the middle of a waving sea of prairie grass. We looked at the neighboring town as if it were no more than a filling station on the road to somewhere else, and the town, in turn, looked at us as if we were an alien legion growing like a cancer on the countryside. The institute's modern, six-story, steel and black-tinted glass structure dominated the rural landscape just outside of Prairie City, and after five years of operation had still never quite managed to fit in. Tall tales were often passed around town, about the sorts of unchristian mayhem that transpired within the institute's complex. But if we were given the abnormal status of some sort of mad scientists' cult, the idea failed to occur to the townspeople that, given the institution's growing size, we were rapidly becoming the majority. Things popped up in town because of our numerous presence—like the Wendy's fast food restaurant, for instance. The townspeople always complained that they were being robbed of their "local flavor" but then without fail you'd be sure to see them eating there with their families later the very same week. To put it plainly: we were the Tribbles that thrived and multiplied when your back was momentarily turned. There was no stopping the momentum of the institute's presence and I think the townspeople knew it from the very beginning.

When I first applied for a position at the institute, in lieu of an interview they administered a series of tests and surveys that combined to form some sort of assessment that might best be described as a twisted-S.A.T.-meets-Cosmo-magazine-quiz-diagnosis. In the end, when it was all over, they shook my hand and welcomed me aboard the team. And, of course, they informed me that my talents would be best harnessed by placing me among the *aesthetics team*. They wanted each and every researcher they hired to find their own special niche and excel in it, they said, and they informed me that I was destined to find mine in the Cosmetic/Rejuvenation department. Consequently, I learned to use my advanced science degrees to create very technologically convincing camouflage. Make-up worth a million bucks. They were right, too—I was really good at my work. I can distill synthetic minerals that can make any wrinkled old bat look a good twenty years younger. I can formulate lotions that hide stretch marks. I can camouflage the world. During my days at the institute, when I would occasionally make the trip to spend the day in Chicago, I'd often see my handiwork go floating past me on the city streets, riding up elevators, or ensconced in the back of a taxicab. It usually caused me to shudder violently, and I found I had a pang of feeling for Don. At the time, I couldn't determine if this pang was sympathy exactly, or perhaps envy. In any case, Don was never made to see somebody wearing his work down Michigan Avenue, and that is the simple truth of the matter.

I'm telling you all of this, of course, because it is important that you understand the circumstances that surrounded Don and me at the time. It is important that you fully comprehend the sort of isolation our environment posed, and how, even with 900 fellow peers it was still possible to feel quite alone. This was the reason why I came to rely on Don's lunchtime companionship, and why I came to look forward to the sixty minutes of my day that we loyally spent together. And finally, this was the reason why, when during his inspection of my newfangled zipper Don's hands passed fleetingly over my chest, I felt a shiver of gooseflesh and I felt my nipples stand up suddenly erect. How embarrassing. I feel I should explain. I feel as though I should have a better defense for my unexpected carnal reaction, but I don't. Don wasn't ordinarily my type—true to my shallow form, I had usually been prone to lusting after the sort of football jocks that warranted the seal of social approval back in my sorority days in college. The guys I dated read *Sports Illustrated* and stored the swimsuit issue on a wicker shelf next to the commode. They spent an inordinate amount of money on their cars and neglected to buy a home computer. They lifted weights and whined about the definition in their abdominal muscles. For some reason or another, I never saw any shame in this. I did, however, find my reaction to Don's floundering hands utterly appalling. How could I justify having such a potent sexual appetite for a man who only I'd only ever heard raise his voice in heated excitement when reading aloud from an article in *Entomologists' Weekly*—an article, I should mention, written about the newly discovered mating habits of the South African Dung Beetle? I still remember that horrific moment with utter clarity, even the precise inflection of Don's voice as he read along. Apparently, the South African Dung Beetle secreted an airborne chemical that had astounding regenerative properties, a chemical akin to the enzyme starfish secreted to regrow their amputated limbs. The only problem was collecting this chemical in a large enough quantity to be studied, as the beetles were quite small and did not release very much during their romantic couplings. Wow, I said to Don—and here I thought starfish were the only ones to produce such an amazing regenerative substance. He cut me off short and quickly corrected me, informing me that it was improper to call them *starfish*. The correct term was *sea star* and only ignorant laymen and small children called them *starfish*. I hushed up shortly after that and concentrated on the careful mastication of my salad.

Now that I have painted you this faint portrait of us, perhaps you can begin to understand my distress. In short, it was degrading to find myself lusting after this man. It was further degrading to instinctively understand that he would never, in a million years, sense my interest nor take any action to meet my demands. Don was merely Don; logical, orderly, efficient, and sterile in every way. There was no tiny seam into his soul, no crack in his countenance through which I might worm my way into his more irrational affections. So this is how it went for quite some time. We ate lunch together on a daily basis, and I watched stray globs of mustard and ketchup slither down his poorly shaved chin, silently wondering what he might do if I just leaned over and licked it up. Inwardly, I scolded myself for thoughts like these, and yet everyday at lunch, I was still palpably compelled to lean over and do something very raunchy to Don. I resigned myself to a polite distance and did nothing.

All that changed, of course, one night when my telephone rang. I almost didn't pick it up—usually the only phone calls I received were from my mother asking why I couldn't find a plane, train, or automobile to carry me the simple distance down to Savannah, Georgia so that I might visit the people who had the good decency to birth me and bring me into God's Green Earth. I dreaded my mother's phone calls, but it had been a good while since her last nagging and I felt it would be only healthy to answer the phone so that I wouldn't weaken my resistance to her pleas by being out of practice. So of course I was shocked, upon answering the phone, to hear a man's voice. It took me several minutes more to realize that it was not only a man's voice, but *Don's voice* on the other end of the phone line. I wracked my brain. Had I given him my number? I must have. Yes, I must have, I decided—for emergencies of course. Did that mean this was an emergency? Why else would he call? I stuttered and um'ed my way through the conversation until at last I realized Don was inviting me somewhere. In fact, he was inviting me over to his townhouse, to be more specific. There was a long pause as I tried to decode this request.

"Are you sick?" I asked, finally.

"No. I'm fine. And even better than that; I've made dinner."

"Dinner?"

"Yes, dinner. I hope you haven't eaten already...?"

"Uh, no."

I stuffed the jumbo bag of potato chips I'd been consuming as my evening meal back into the pantry, hoping Don couldn't hear the crinkling noises of the bag over the phone.

"Good. It's 223 Eden Drive. Come as soon as it's convenient."

He hung up. No goodbye, no elaboration, just the invitation and an address. Eden Drive; I looked on a map and saw that Eden Drive was outside of Prairie City, in one of the new suburban developments that had cropped up to accommodate the town's new influx of population. It was a private, gated community, and mostly people from the institute lived there. The development also included a country club and golf course, and also a series of man-made lakes. I saw that Eden Drive backed up right along one of these lakes. I traced a finger over the roads that led from my apartment to Eden Drive, memorizing the route. Then I flipped my road atlas shut and raced to the bathroom. At this point, I am ashamed to say, a flurry of ridiculous grooming ensued. I fired up a curling iron. I stripped down to my underwear and lathered my legs with shaving cream. I extracted cosmetic products from my makeup bag that hadn't seen daylight in almost a decade. I rolled a little furry brush of jet-black mascara through my lashes. I applied shimmering pink gloss to my lips with a tiny paintbrush. I spritzed myself with Chanel No.5 and stepped into a dress. I bravely slipped on a pair of high heels I'd rarely worn in the past for fear of vertigo. Teetering as if on stilts, I paused and took a good look in the full-length mirror hanging on the back of my closet door. It was all very surreal, and I dashed out of my apartment barely recognizing the girl I saw in the mirror.

When I pulled up in front of 223 Eden Drive, I took a deep breath and cut the motor of my car. I noted that the lake I had spotted on the map was concealed from view. The houses must line up along the shore, I decided, endless rows of sliding glass doors facing out to take in all the man-made glory of the lake. I drew up to the front door and rang the bell. Don answered quickly, throwing the door open and waving an arm to gesture me inside. I stepped through the doorway, and cast a quick look about my surroundings. There was a distinct dorm-room feeling to Don's townhouse. The furniture looked as if it had been ordered all in one sitting from an IKEA catalogue. Most of the wall-hangings took the form of unframed posters.

Peeking into an adjacent room I spotted a giant Periodic Table and a huge saltwater aquarium.

"What took you so long?" he asked with his back to me as I shut the front door and followed the silhouette of his retreating form toward the dining room. He turned to face me and pulled out a dining room chair so that I might sit. He took no notice whatsoever of my dress, my shoes, my diligently applied lip gloss.

"Oh, um, I don't know. I was in the middle of something when you called."

To this he did not reply. He shuffled some things about on the dining room table and poured the wine. I sniffed my glass and judged it to be a nicely robust cabernet sauvignon. A very romantic wine, I privately thought, but tried not to read too much into my observations.

"Wait here," he commanded, and disappeared into the kitchen. He returned several moments later with two plates of risotto and creamed spinach and a heavy crock-pot. He set the crock-pot down in the center of the table. I watched it steam and the air around us was instantly filled with a delicious aromatic scent.

"Mmm," I said, appreciatively looking the wine-soaked juices in the crock-pot, "Looks like braised short ribs."

"Yes. Pretty much, with carrots, celery and onions." Don replied. He picked up a large serving spoon and ladled a generous helping onto my plate. He settled back into his own chair, pulling a napkin into his lap. "Dig in."

Obediently, I cut a morsel from the bone and scooped it up with some of the vegetables, savoring it slowly. It was wonderful; the meat was rich and savory, and had obviously been slow cooked in the crock-pot for several hours. I looked over at my companion, whose face was turned down into his plate of food, happily gobbling away. I watched him affectionately for a moment, bemused with his child-like vigor. I had not pegged Don for a kitchen-savvy chef. Perhaps there was more to his personality than I knew—perhaps this dinner was a signal that he was finally ready to reveal a more personal side of himself to me. My mind began to stray, reeling with questions. Did he prepare such elaborate meals for himself? Or was this meal specially prepared in my honor? This dish implied serious premeditation, but the invitation only came at the last minute. Had he planned on calling me all along?

Suddenly I realized that Don had ceased eating. He had eaten his dinner with alarming speed. The stew on his plate was all gone, though stray globs of risotto and spinach remained. He was watching me, an intensity burning in his eyes that I had never seen before. Unable to desist from shoveling forkfuls of the addictive braise into my mouth, I continued to eat under his heavy gaze. I ate with gusto, and my voracious appetite seemed only to spur my companion on, a devilish smile spreading across Don's face with every bite I took. Eventually, as I neared my last mouthful of stew, Don rose from his seat abruptly, knocking the dining room chair over in the process. He rushed over to me, and without uttering a word he took me by the wrist and led me from the dining room to the living room. Shocked by this unfamiliar behavior, I followed his lead silently. He sunk into a leather armchair and pulled me over to him so that I was straddled astride his lap. We looked at one another for a moment, temporarily frozen, and I thought I saw the dark pupils of Don's eyes dilate like a wild animal's. Then, as if pulled together by a sudden suction of air, our mouths quickly found each other, licking and gulping in an almost panicked frenzy. Don reached a hand down between our writhing bodies and I felt his hands along my sides, sliding my dress up to my waist. My head was spinning; I tried to get my bearings. I guess I had imagined it differently, more fumbling and awkward maybe. I hadn't counted on Don being so sexually aggressive. Our bodies rose and fell together in waves and I had a sense of potent dizziness. Leaning my head back, I opened my eyes and noticed a peculiar pair of portraits hanging on the wall over the fireplace. It was James T. Kirk and Mr. Spock, done in oil paints.

When it was over, we sat still pretzeled together in a crumpled heap of hair and sweat on the leather chair for an unimaginable length of time. Finally Don scooped me up, carrying me through a hallway into his bedroom. He laid me gently down on the bed and hovered over me, his shape now seeming new and strange to me. Methodically, he very slowly removed my shoes, my dress, my stockings, my garter belt, and my underwear. What happy luck I had suddenly stumbled upon! I must have known subconsciously, I thought to myself, that Don would be such an avid, adept lover. I sighed contentedly, grateful that my bizarre attraction had finally been explained and justified.

"Wait," I said playfully. "That's no fair."

"What do you mean?"

"I'm the only one naked."

"So?"

"So you have to get naked too."

He sighed, slightly frustrated. Flirtatiously, I slid the fountain pens out of his shirt pocket, one by one, and giggled, throwing them onto the floor. Then I began to unbutton his white, short-sleeved dress shirt, pulling the shirttails out of his pants. I slid off his undershirt and pressed my cool hands over the hot, clammy skin of his chest, pausing to kiss his nipples. Then I noticed something wrong, something strangely different. I blinked in astonishment. I couldn't believe it. There were huge red scars along both sides of his rib cage. An accident or series of operations, I thought? But the wounds looked so fresh.

"Don—you never told me..."

"Oh, that," he said, as though it were no big deal. "That's only temporary."

"What do you mean?" I asked, daring to run a shy finger over the bumpy stitched surface. He exhaled heavily and rolled over to lie next to me on the bed.

"I guess I should tell you."

"Tell me what?"

"Well," he began, his voice hesitant and careful, "you know the research I've been working on?"

"Of course."

"Well, it worked."

"What do you mean 'it worked?' You found a way to use starfish enzymes for human medicine?"

"Not starfish. *Sea stars.*"

"Sorry—I forget. *Sea stars,* then. Whatever. You found a way to use their enzymes?"

Don smiled widely, looking at me from the side of his eyes.

"I have," he said smugly. "Soon my ribcage will be back to its normal condition. You'll see."

I pondered this a moment, confused. There was just one thing I could not reconcile within my own mind. I cleared my throat and summoned my courage.

"Don, can I ask… where did you get those scars in the first place?"

To my surprise, he began to chuckle in a low voice. I reached an arm over his shoulder and shook him gently, but he erupted into an outright peel of laughter. I narrowed my eyes at him.

"I'm sorry. I'm not laughing at you."

"What are you laughing at then?" I demanded, not amused in the slightest.

"Well, it's just that, I made those incisions, for my research."

I shot up in the bed, grabbing for a pillow to cover my chest, which had suddenly grown very cold.

"Oh my god, Don. You're insane. You could have killed yourself. And what if things don't work out? What if your body is disfigured for life? Do you honestly think you can just chop into your flesh and have it magically heal?"

Don just laughed, riled on by my hysterical ranting. I looked at him and recoiled. I was suddenly revolted with myself. I couldn't believe I had just made love to this lunatic.

"You need help," I said, picking up my clothes from the floor and pulling them back on.

"Wait," he said, reaching after me and resting a hand on my bare back. "C'mon. You're overreacting. It's not like I woke up one morning and just decided to do this. You know me. I wouldn't do anything so irrational."

I looked at him sternly, not saying a word.

"I started small and worked my way up to this point."

"You started small?" I echoed, totally baffled by this new admission. "What does that mean?"

"It means I started small. Literally. You know—the tips of fingers and toes and that sort of thing. I'm happy to report that I've been able to regrow every single bit of flesh that's been removed."

"Are you serious?" I stuttered. Momentarily I considered the possibility that Don was yanking my chain. In the past, Don had never possessed much of a sense of humor, but tonight he didn't sound or seem at all like his normal self. Anything seemed possible.

"Are you serious?" I repeated.

"Totally serious. I've been at this a long time."

"How long?"

"Oh, months. That's why I finally invited you over to dinner tonight," he said, his tone light and conversational. "My freezer was getting a little backed up. It's been chock full for weeks now, so I had to do something."

Do something??? The words echoed in my ears. My blood ran cold. What did his freezer have to do with it?

"Jesus, Don. You didn't."

"Well I can't go around dumping body parts in the trash. Even considering they're my own, the police might think that was rather strange of me. I deemed consumption to be the most convenient means of disposal."

I stood frozen next to the bed, my panties on and my bra not yet fastened. Don sat on the edge of the bed, facing me. He reached up and slid his hands down to the hourglass of my waist. He leaned forward and kissed my bare stomach.

"I should tell you, I was quite turned on watching you eat this evening."

I felt nauseous. Blood was pounding in my head. My throat constricted.

"Don," my voice came out hard and flat. "What did I eat?"

"What else?" he smiled and flicked his tongue into my belly button. He looked up to peer at me. "My ribs."

"Ohmigod." I reached a hand to my mouth as if to stop the sensation of vomit rising in my throat. I snatched my clothes up from the floor and turned to run from the room desperately, half naked and blind with horror. I ran through the hallways of Don's townhouse, suddenly confused about which direction to run. I ran stupidly, without knowing where I was headed and not caring. I felt my feet leave the carpet and patter loudly across a hardwood floor. I knew, somehow, I was in the kitchen. I stopped, suddenly paralyzed. I could vaguely hear Don laughing from the bedroom, but it was muffled, as if someone had put their hands over my ears. I looked around, feeling sick and dirty and helpless. Then I spotted the refrigerator. It was as if the refrigerator glared at me, its motor hummed loudly, a slight rattling coming from its lower grill. My frozen muscles relaxed, suddenly certain of what was to be done. I moved very carefully, taking long, deliberate steps. Slowly I reached a hand out, then proceeded to tug firmly at the freezer door.

When I opened the freezer door, I did not shriek, I did not gasp, and I did not faint. Instead, I very calmly extracted a heavy package of meat, walked over to the sliding glass door and let myself out onto Don's back patio. The night was windless, and the lake looked very calm. At opposite ends of the lake, there were two spouts of water, jetting proudly into the air, lit up with colored floodlights. The moon was full and its reflection shone like a mirror in the surface of the water, even the purplish-gray craters discernable. Still naked and shivering, I dropped my clothes on the patio and grasped the package with two hands. I spun around as if I were throwing a discus in the Olympics, and I heaved it as far out into the lake as it could possibly go, then pulled on my clothes to go. When I looked back over my shoulder, I glimpsed the package as it capsized and sunk. Ironically, it was to be the last I saw of Don.

—

In the days that followed, I quit my job at the institution without giving notice and took a position as a toxicologist out in California. I worked for the state, and mostly ran drug screenings for various state agencies. It wasn't interesting work, but it was straightforward and the hours were regular. Eventually, I moved into a suburban development called Fairvale and my days passed quickly under the benign sunshine of season-less California. I made house payments, washed my car with the garden hose, and mowed my lawn on Sundays—just like all my neighbors did. I never spoke to anyone about Don or his strange experiments, but I thought about it often. Why had I been so horrified? Wasn't Don just trying to make the world a better place? I mean, if you thought about it, the idea that humans could consume and regenerate their own flesh might one day mean the end of world hunger. And yet, there was something within me that still violently protested every time I pictured that steaming crock-pot on Don's dining room table. When I thought of this, I flinched and tried to put the image out of my mind. Usually I was quite successful in my voluntary amnesia.

There was one small item of unfinished business, however. A month after I moved to California, I received a phone call from the Illinois State Police. It seemed a gruesome package of ribs positively identified as human had been discovered in a local community lake. The police could not identify the owner and were worried that the rest of the body had been dismembered and scattered about at different locations. Since my license plate had been recorded at the visitor's gate that night, they needed to ask me a few questions about my whereabouts. I told the officer on the phone that I had gone to see a coworker who lived at 223 Eden Drive.

"Oh, yes—Donald Prescott. Yep. Looks like we already interviewed him and he said he was entertaining a lady friend that evening. That must be you."

"You already spoke to Don?"

"Yeah. It looks like both of your stories check out. Sorry to have bothered you ma'am. Best of luck to you out there in California."

Abruptly, the officer hung up. I stood there, holding the phone, momentarily entranced. They had already spoken to Don, and had noticed nothing suspicious. Suddenly I burst out laughing. What did I expect? That the police would know to take a sample of Don's DNA and match it to the meat in the package? Why on earth would they suspect that Don had anything to do with it? After all, Don probably looked fine and healthy by now, and no reason to rouse anybody's suspicion.

Even under the warm California sun I couldn't help but shiver as the thought ran through my mind: all the police had to go on was a rack of ribs.

Kitchen Communion

Camilla Trinchieri

Mama has been cooking for a solid week. The food we eat during this week of mourning must be hers only. When Sal tried to go down the road to get doughnuts, Mama stopped him at the door. "I'll make you doughnuts that'll make your belly sing. No hole, that's a waste of good dough. If you need the hole, cut it out yourself."

She is grieving, she is not herself, we, her three children, tell each other with glances behind her back. We sit at the round kitchen table by the bay window for breakfast, lunch and dinner, like the old days when we were still a family gathered under one roof. Foods that marked the Sundays of our growing up, that came from every region of Italy: from Campania where Mama was born: *Calamari in Umido, Maccheroni con Carciofi* from Calabria, lamb *alla Bolognese* from Emilia-Romagna, *Capretto* with fava beans from Lazio.

We eat; we thank her for the bounty of her table; we think we know what she is up to. Mama is weighing us down, hoping she can anchor us to this house, bring us back to filial duty, to respect, maybe even to loving our father.

Her back to us, mama stands on the solid wooden box Papa made for her so that she can reach the sink and the stove. She has just come home from Mass and is still wearing her blue straw hat with the veil pushed up as high as a crown. I rub Mama's back, tight with unhappiness, as she shucks the peas.

"Let me," I offer. Mama elbows me away and wraps the sheet of newspaper around the empty pea shells. Beef broth is simmering on the back burner. Diced onion and pancetta wait on the cutting board. Today we will lunch on *Risi e Bisi* to honor the trickle of Venetian blood in Pap's veins, a northern heritage of which he boasted to every Italian-American he met.

Mike, the oldest, the one Papa hit on the hardest, lights a cigarette. "So what are we going to do with Papa's ashes?" After lunch we are heading home—me to Brooklyn, Mike two roads down from Mama, Sal way across the country—each of us to our own hideout, away from the shrinking walls of our house.

Mama turns around to face us, the glasses she need for her nearsightedness still in place. We are blurs to her. She has not taken off her glasses since Papa dropped dead last Saturday, fitting an Armani suit at Garden City's Saks for an old customer of his.

"Burning your father!" She is still on her box with her fist buried between her breasts, as if she'd grown a hole there. Her eyes are fixed with a new determination—eyes that can turn sweet a sudden memory, at a kindness or a touch from one of us. Radiant eyes when papa was anywhere near her. "You're real happy about that. You think you're clever ganging up on me."

"We didn't twist your arm," I say.

"We've been over this a thousand times." Mike opens the window wider. I hand him a small coffee cup to use as an ashtray. Outside in the vegetable garden mama has cut down the row of Easter lilies. The stubs look hacked.

"The Vatican says that cremation is okay," Sal says. He opens the refrigerator that is filled with Mama's leftovers. The food the neighborhood women brought the first few days Mama made me take over to Our Lady of Divine Grace.

"They're doing it in Italy now, too." Sal helps himself to a cold slice of eggplant from yesterday's parmigiana. "I guess they ran out of room, huh?" He pops another slice in his mouth.

"Wait for dinner, Sal." Mama's words come out weary from having been repeated for most of Sal's life.

"Cremation is what he wanted, okay?" Mike blows smoke toward the open window. "He told me he didn't want a fuss."

Mama hunches her shoulders, drops them suddenly, as if their weight has caught her unawares. "He said nothing to me."

"He didn't always tell you everything. I'm his first son. I'm the one he told."

We got Mama to agree to cremate Papa with a lie; he didn't tell his first son, second son or daughter anything. Papa wasn't a communicator. Cremating Papa was our decision. It seemed simpler, more cost efficient, the American thing to do.

"We executed his wishes." Mike's voice is loud now. The only other sound is a far off mower. "That's what we did, and all you do is lay down a guilt trip."

"Hey Mike, control the foghorn, okay?" Sal says. He looks as if he's ready to give Mike a fast kick in the pants. Sal, obedient, respectful, was Papa's golden boy until he exchanged the sun of Long Island for California's Silicon Valley and forever happy skies. He can do no wrong for Mama. "And no smoking in the house, okay?"

Mike drags harder on his cigarette between swigs of his beer.

Mama gets off the box and kicks it closer to the stove to swirl butter in the hot pan. She adds a little olive oil. "To stop the butter from burning," she used to tell me when she was still trying to teach me what I refused to learn. "Cooking, that's how you hold a family together," she'd add in hopes of snaring my interest. It was the first disappointment I gave her.

I watch her throw in the onion and pancetta and wonder if she has seen through our lie. "He loved you Mama," I say. "He didn't want to keep you tied to him after his death." No headstone demanding weekly visits with flowers and prayers as if it were some altar.

"You," Mama sweeps the handle of the pan across the room to include the three of us. "You don't want to come back to pay your respects!"

I say, "Remember Rita Cerani's husband dead three weeks, she put her head in the oven and turned on the gas? That night at the beach after her funeral? You remember that?" It was a summer night, the kitchen too hot to cook in, and Papa had come up with the idea of dinner on the beach. While the boys and Papa gathered driftwood, Mama and I unpacked the pots and the dishes from the trunk of the car.

"When I die, don't do anything crazy," he said, shaking the skillet closer to the fire to nudge the clams open. "And I want no black, you hear, Connie? Wait a couple of months, then dress yourself up and catch yourself a new young man. To hell with what the neighbors think."

Mama laughed and hugged his arm. "If you go, I'll decide what to wear, not you." She kissed him then, on the lips, the firelight licking their joined faces, leaving a glow. When they parted the tip of Mama's tongue disappeared back into the darkness of her mouth as if it was a candy she was eager to suck. It was the longest, most embarrassing moment of my ten-year-old existence. Later I asked Sal if it was the mention of death that sexed Mama up. He said dumb questions didn't deserve answers, but I swore to myself never to bring up the subject of death anywhere near a boy.

"We could borrow Vito's boat and scatter Papa in the ocean," Sal says. "He might even float all the way to Italy and get to visit finally." Papa felt there was never enough money for them to go. When the bank promoted me to assistant treasurer two years ago, I offered to them the trip. Papa was too stubborn and proud to accept.

"They don't scatter in Italy," Mama says. She hands me the knives and forks for me to set the table. She shakes her head when I hand them over to Sal. The same thing happens when I hand over the dishes, her good Sunday dishes that have to be washed by hand.

"We can bury the urn in the rose bushes," Sal offers. "Papa can stay in one place, if that's what you want."

"He loved those roses," I add.

"Is this a religious thing?" Mike asks, his elbows rooted to the table Sal is trying to set. The tablecloth, Papa's wedding gift to Mama, has been in place since our first meal together after the funeral. White linen with white roses embroidered in the corners, it comes out for special occasions and she has never let a stain stay on it for more than a couple of hours. Now it's covered with this past week's food spatterings. I offered to pay for a trip to the cleaners more than once, but Mama insists it's just fine the way it is. She won't even let me change the napkins, Mama who was called *Santa Netezza* by Papa, Saint Clean.

"She wants to make that tablecloth unrecognizable," Sal said this morning when we cleared the breakfast dishes. "She's hell-bent on destroying it. I bet you the next time you come she'll have thrown it away."

I scratched at the crust of a tomato stain with my nail. Maybe she wants to keep a record of this week. The three of us with her, eating through her grief."

Mike scrunches his cigarette down into the coffee cup. "Are you worried about the Second Coming?" he asks Mama. "The resurrection bit, the body has to be whole to make it to Heaven. Is that it?"

"You don't even respect your father after he's dead and can't do you any harm." Mama's body shakes as her elbow rises and falls with each stir of the rice. "You wanted to make sure there'd be nothing left of him." Whatever he did, he didn't deserve that." She steps down from her box and pours the *Risi e Bisi* into the Capo di Monte tureen Vito Marinucci brought back for my parents after a trip to Naples. Vito was Papa's best friend and offered the luncheon after the funeral at his restaurant the Sea Palace, with its three banquet halls dripping glass from the ceilings and a view of the Sound from the ladies' room. Mama invited all the old timers I the neighborhood and the salesmen from the men's department at Saks. Mike was angry at her for accepting Vito's generosity. "We aren't beggars," he kept repeating during the luncheon. "We could have had it at the Plaza." Mike does handiwork for a living and barely scrapes by.

Mama takes off her apron, makes her way to the table, holding the tureen. Mike gets up to get another beer. Sal pulls out the chair for her.

"Don't worry about your father," Mama says. "I'm taking care of him."

"Your hat," I remind her as she's about to sit down. She takes it off with a shaky smile, the first of the week, and hands it to me.

"It's been ten years since we sat together, all of us at one table," she says. It's a statement of fact. She is done with reproaches.

Mike sits back down and glances at his watch. "It's been four and a half hours. At breakfast."

"That's not what Mama means," Sal says, sitting down next to her.

"He knows what I mean," Mama says.

My place is next to Papa's empty chair, which I don't take because suddenly I don't know what to do with my feet or Mama's hat. I'm back to being twelve, at another Sunday lunch in this kitchen:

"You've got a wife and three kids," Mama says to Papa's stony face. I'm the only kid there. Sal and Mike are at the beach. Papa's long hand twirls spaghetti around his fork. His thumb is covered with needle pricks from sewing. Thimbles are for sissies. He works the fork so quickly bits of sauce fly out and spatter on my blouse.

"You've got a wife and three kids," she repeats.

"What are you talking about?" Papa asks.

"You know what I mean."

Papa's fingers don't stop turning until he's got every strand tightly wound. Nothing else is said.

After an afternoon spent working on his roses, Papa moved out. He came back three years later, while I was painting my nails fuchsia at the kitchen table and Mama was cooking dinner. Without even looking at him Mama said, "Hurry and wash up, I just threw in the pasta."

I still have the bottle of fuchsia nail polish.

—

Mama takes off her glasses and wave her hand at me. "Louisa, just put down the hat and sit down."

We shake out our napkins in unison. "Get ready," Papa would say as we sat down at the table, our napkins in our fists. "Get set," he continued to say after he came back. "Go!" And we, his kids, continued to play along, allowing him this one family game. Unfurling my napkin is as familiar and unconscious a motion as crossing myself when I walk into a church. A commemoration of sorts to a man I stopped believing in.

Mama's head barely clears the reclining figure of Neptune on the lid of the tureen. Our plates are piled next to her elbow, waiting to be filled. She clasps her hands. For a second I think she's going to pray.

"Family stays with you," she says, "even after you goof to lead your own lives, even after death. That's the way it is, like it or not. You think you're better than him, that you're not going to make any mistakes in your life. He's dead and you've gotten rid of him, dust to dust and all that baloney. Wrong! Your father's in your blood and he'll be in your children's blood if you should be so lucky to get married and have some. And you're the better for it." She lifts up the lid of the dish. A veil of steam covers her face. "It's you he came back to. He loved you with everything he had and I want you to keep that love. It'll make life good for you, believe me. A mother's wish. Now *buon appetito.*"

"*Buon appetito,*" we repeat together, our amen of the table, as she ladles out the creamy rice. The steam has evaporated and the air smells sweet of peas and butter. White ocean light reaches into our corner snatching the gloom from our faces. I flatten the rice into a circle and start from the cool edge of the plate. It's delicious, as always. Vito claims Mama's the best cook this side of the Atlantic. I think Papa came back for her cooking.

Sal watches me eat and laughs. "The map, Mama. We can't eat *Risi e Bisi* without the map."

"Right behind Louisa."

I turn around. The boot of Italy stares back at me, each region colored in a different color by me more than twenty years ago. Campagna is yellow because Mama claims that is where the sun shines brightest. She remembers the light even though she left when she was three years old. The light of Long Island comes closest, she says.

Through food we discovered the old country. Every Saturday morning, while Mama cleaned the house and my brothers played baseball with the neighborhood boys, Papa would take down the map of Italy and put it out on the table between us. I would close my eyes and let my finger fall on a region. Sometimes I cheated and kept one eye half open to make sure I didn't pick last week's place. For the next half hour before Papa had to leave for work, we would go through cookbooks and recipes Mama had gotten from neighbors or copied down from the books in the library. At Sunday's big meal, while we ate the region's specialty, Papa or Mama would give us a history lesson.

I recite what I remember. "Venice was built on 117 islands by people fleeing the barbarians. During the Middle Ages and the Renaissance Lombardy was important for banking and today it boasts the largest production of silk. Apulia is famous for its pink Baroque buildings and the strange white trulli with conical roofs no one can explain."

Mama nods her head in approval. She is filling our plates again.

"I remember the food," Mike says, leaning back into the window, letting the sun relax his face. "Duck stuffed with chicken livers and mushrooms."

"Calabria," Sal says. "How about those fried cookies? *Panelle?*"

"From Sardinia. Made with chick pea flour." My favorite region was Sicily. Pasta *a sfinciuni* followed by sword fish *rustutu cú sammurigghiú*, the words as exotic as the tastes were strong.

Mama looks into the Capo di Monte tureen. It is empty and her face folds in, like those flowers that close up at the end of the day. "*Risi e Bisi* comes with a poem Papa wrote. Who remembers it?" She keeps her head down, as if expecting the silence that follows.

I get up, taking Mama's hat with me, and walk to the hallway. I hang the hat on a peg next to her coat while my eyes travel to the door of my parent's bedroom. Pap's urn is in there. I walk on tiptoe, an old habit. The door is locked. Never in all those years growing up did they lock their door. I used to think, when sex grew heavy on my mind, that the unlocked door was the reason Papa left. I tiptoe back to the front door and get Mama's keys from her coat pocket.

Papa's urn is resting on the bedside table that Mama has moved to the foot of the bed directly in line with her pillow. Surrounding the table, the lilies from the garden, each in its own vase, look like wobbly candelabras. Their perfume is overpowering. I feel like a gag has been pressed against my nose and mouth. I want to get out of there, but instead I sit down on the bed and stare at the copper urn, burnished so that fingerprints won't show. "So that faces of ungrateful children will not show either," I imagine Papa saying. I'm not proud of myself.

After Papa came back, Sal and Mike were old enough to be able to ignore the rules he tried to reinstate. They tolerated him for Mama's sake, without showing either anger or love. I became ashamed of him, the feeling growing stronger every day, making me leave home a month after I graduated from high school. I told myself I was ashamed of finding him hunched down on a kitchen stool in his long-sleeved woolen undershirt, soaking his feet after work. I was ashamed of the way he'd take out his measuring tape in front of my friends to make sure my skirt was two inches below the knee, of the way he'd lift the lids off the pots cooking on the stove to taste Mama's cooking and tell her add salt or water, to lower or increase the flame, as if she couldn't perfect a dish without him. Above all, I was ashamed of myself for not being able to keep Papa home.

I tap the urn's lid, a friendly pat like the one Papa used to give the top of my head as I'd fly across the room on the way to school, to friends, to the beach, his way of registering my passage through his space. Now he's the one who's flown through my life in what seems a blink of the eye. I guess he was a good man. Mama says he loved us. I don't know. I'd like to believe it, but I'm scared of the grief that would come with that. I give him another tap. It's the best I can do fro now. I've been unable to cry.

The lid shifts under my hand. The urn has been opened. My eye catches a trail of dirt on the crocheted cover of the table.

Lifting the urn, I find it much lighter than the five pounds I carried home from the funeral parlor. The dirt on the table disintegrates into silken ash when I dab it with a finger. I open the urn slowly, afraid Papa might spill over me. It's half empty. I put the urn back at the center of the table and screw the lid on tightly.

What has Mama done with him? The week's litany of food comes back to me, her insistence that we stay the week, that let her cook all our meals. Slowly, unbelievingly, I get it.

In the bathroom I try to throw up, but nothing come out and I sit on the toilet bowl and wait, in case my stomach changes its mind. I lean back against the cool porcelain of the tank and debate telling my brothers. I can see Mike sticking his finger down his throat, his face flashing the anger he can barely contain under any circumstances. He would never forgive Mama.

Sal laughing. "Holy communion," he might say. "This is his body. This is his blood. Cool."

As the minutes pass I realize that dusting our food with Papa's ashes makes a crazy sort of sense, Mama's way of keeping the family intact.

"You fall in?" Mike asks when I get back to the kitchen.

"How could you forget the poem?" Mama is asking Sal as he makes espresso on the machine Sal and I bought our parents on their fortieth wedding anniversary. The house is filled with our collective guilt at having walked away. "Your father wrote it for you kids."

He didn't write it; just translated it from the Italian he found in a cookbook at Vito Marinucci's house. I have the same cookbook that's how I know. I drop Mama's keys on the table.

163

She casts her eyes down, then lifts them to search my face, with the same look of worry she had when came home from school, always on the lookout for a fever or a humiliation on our faces. I kiss the top of Mama's head and start reciting.

> *"To bless the holy spring*
> *That makes a garden nice*
> *All I need is a bowl*
> *A bowl of peas and rice."*

Mama's eyes turn sweet. That's when I ask her if there are any leftovers for me to take home.

RECIPES

Thyestian Feast
Take two young boys and remove the hands and feet. Reserve these for taunting their father later. Lay some filo dough in a broad casserole and butter generously. Line with a mixture of spinach, crumbled feta and eggs. Place pieces of the boys on top, and cover with more dough, well buttered. Bake in a moderate oven at 400 degrees for one hour, until the edges are crisp and the boys are cooked through. In Greek this is called Ago'ripita. Serve to dad. But be prepared for revenge, when dad sleeps with his daughter and their son kills you in turn.

Ken Albala

Medieval Bone Bread
Smell your Englishman well to be sure he isn't French or German (which will make an inferior crust). Carefully remove the flesh by holding the head firmly and biting down on the rest of the body and draw slowly between your massive teeth. Clean the remaining bones and grind them well in a mortar and pestle with blanched almonds and a few drops of rosewater. Add fresh ale-yeast, the yolk of one egg, a pinch of saffron and a quintal of finest flour and enough water to make a firm dough. Knead well and let rise in a warm place until doubled in bulk. Bake in a hot oven for 45 minutes. Eat hot with black puddings.

Ken Albala

JUST DESSERTS

"I have been assured by a very knowing American of my acquaintance in London, that a young healthy child, well nursed, is, at a year old, a most delicious, nourishing and wholesome food, whether stewed, roasted, baked or boiled; and I make no doubt that it will equally serve in a fricassee or a ragout."
Jonathan Swift, "A Modest Proposal"

FRIENDS FOR DINNER

Jeri Quinzio

MENU

Finger Foods
Lady's Thigh Meatballs
Swaddled Babies

Bloody Mary or Virgin Mary

First Course
Little Ears with Tomato Sauce
Buttered Bastards

Blood of Judas

Main Course
Glasgow Magistrates
Moors and Christians
Dead Fingers, Penises & Testicles

Tears of Christ

Desserts
Virgin's Breasts
Chancellor's Buttocks
Mother-in-Law's Tongues

Milk of our Blessed Mother

After Dinner
Bones of the Dead
Corpse Revivers

Having friends for dinner makes most hosts and hostesses a little anxious, no matter how often they entertain. We worry about how the recipes will turn out, whether guests will be allergic to or simply dislike something we serve, and whether they'll reject an unfamiliar dish. But this menu was such a success with my friends that I hope you'll try it with yours.

We started with finger foods in the living room. I passed trays laden with delectably tender Lady's Thigh Meatballs as well as scrumptious little Swaddled Babies. We sipped Bloody Marys or Virgin Marys.

Then, seated in the dining room, we nibbled on a first course of Little Ears, tender yet with some tooth to them, served with tomato sauce. With them, we ate Buttered Bastards and drank the Blood of Judas.

The main course was Glasgow Magistrates, and what chubby, well-fed magistrates they must have been. But there was much more. An ample dish of Moors and Christians, peacefully together at last. Some perfectly prepared Dead Fingers. Spicy Penises, always popular with those who like a little heat, were accompanied by some unctuous sliced Testicles. We drank the Tears of Christ.

I had picked up an array of delicacies for dessert at my neighborhood bakery. My own favorites, a rare and wondrous treat, were the Virgin's Breasts. Others preferred the richer, plumper Chancellor's Buttocks, or the Mother-in-Law's Tongues, which were surprisingly sweet and not surprisingly very crisp. With the desserts, we drank the Milk of our Blessed Mother.

A few night owls stayed up after most of the guests had gone, munching on crunchy little Bones of the Dead and sipping Corpse Revivers until well after the witching hour.

Okay. This is not a gathering of people who dine on people. The menu items are simply named for bodies, body parts, or bodily emanations. But what is in a name? No one knows why so many foods are named after body parts. Are the names a charm against cannibalism or an echo of it? Are they intended as harmless fun or to ward off evil? Do they represent Hansel and Gretel or Hannibal Lecter?

Consider the above menu. The Lady's Thigh Meatballs are a Turkish dish, *Kadinbudu Köfte*, a mixture of minced meat and rice shaped into small slender ovals and fried. They are supposed to be shaped like graceful ladies' thighs. A slightly different mixture, shaped into smaller, more elongated ovals, is called *Kuru Köfte* or Fried Meat Fingers.

The Swaddled Baby appetizer we chose was from the Dominican Republic. Called *Niño Envuelto* in Spanish, it's a rice cake wrapped in cabbage leaves. A Mexican omelet wrapped around a seafood mixture is known by the same name. Both recall the days when infants were wrapped in swaddling clothes, although neither explains why we would want to replicate them in food.

The drinks were a Bloody Mary, which may or may not have been named for the sixteenth-century British queen, but is certainly known for its rich blood-red color. It's made with tomato juice, vodka, and spicy seasonings. The Virgin Mary is the same drink sans vodka. They're not the only drinks that sound like a vampire's dream. There's also a Bloody Maria with tequila substituting for vodka, as well as a Blood and Sand, a Bloody Brew, and a Bloody Bull.

Our first course of Little Ears is *Orecchiette*, one of many pastas named for body parts. With a little imagination, their small, rounded shapes do look like tiny ears. *Orecchioni* are large ears. We all know elbow macaroni, *gomiti* in Italian. There's also *linguine*, or little tongues, and *mostaccioli*, little mustaches. Angel's hair pasta, *capelli d'angelo*, is fine and delicate and extremely popular—as is the even wispier *capellini*. There's also the thin, curly pasta called *capieddi è pretti,* or priest's hair. Apparently priests in Calabria have thin, curly hair.

Claudia Roden describes a jam called *confiture de cheveux d'ange,* angel hair jam, in *A Book of Jewish Food*. She makes it from spaghetti squash and says it's a Syrian specialty.

Hot, golden dogfish fillets that curl up when they're smoked are popular beer garden snacks in Germany. They're called *Schillerlocken* for the eighteenth-century poet Johann von Schiller's curly locks, according to Martha Barnette's book *Ladyfingers & Nun's Tummies*.

The Chinese drink a tea called Old Man's Eyebrows. And we cannot forget (much as we might like to) the cocktail known as a Hairy Navel, made of peach schnapps, vodka, and orange juice. Without the vodka, it's just a Fuzzy Navel.

Our Buttered Bastard was, of course, a *Bâtard* or loaf of French bread. Traditionally it's the same weight as a baguette, but shorter, squatter, and less elegant. Perhaps it's a bastardized version of the classic French bread. With our ears and bastards we drank an Italian red wine from Lombardy called *Sangue di Giuda* or Blood of Judas.

The main course, Glasgow Magistrates, is a dish of Loch Fyne herrings that are so rotund they call to mind courtroom officials, according to Jane Garmey, author of *Great British Cooking*. Another good choice would have been Curate's Cheek, a British dish of ham baked with mustard, sugar, and cream. Or we could have had Fat Monks, *Monacone*, a Caprese casserole made with layers of eggplant, veal, prosciutto, Fontina, and tomatoes. Rich, substantial dishes are named for well-fed, full-bodied people with good reason. Who'd want to eat anything called, say, Runway Model or Preteen Gymnast?

The Tears of Christ we drank with the Glasgow Magistrates is better known as *Lachryma Christi*. It's a crisp, dry white (there's also a red) from the slopes of Mount Vesuvius. Legend has it that when Jesus was saddened by acts of the devil He cried, and grapevines sprang up where His tears fell. Thus, the tears of Christ.

As for the accompaniments, Moors and Christians, *Moros y Christianos*, is a Cuban dish of black beans and rice named for its black and white colors. The phrase is also the name of an annual Spanish festival, during which people dress up, pretend to fight old battles, and then celebrate together.

Dead Fingers, *Dooie Vingers* in Dutch, is a preparation of long, pale stalks of kohlrabi. There are many foods named Ladies' Fingers. In the nineteenth century, the name was given to some varieties of vegetables and fruits including okra, potatoes, bananas, and grapes. There's at least one cocktail called a Lady Finger. It's made with gin, kirschwasser and cherry brandy. Most other finger foods are sweets.

I'm puzzled at the lack of toe foods. Toes, at least babies' toes, are plump and cute; one would expect lots of foods to be named after them. I thought Tootsie Rolls might qualify, but the candy was so called because the maker's daughter was nicknamed Tootsie. On the other hand, feet are seldom attractive, yet in Northern England a regional variation on the Cornish Pasty is called Lancashire Foot and shaped like one.

—

The appearance of some foods does call to mind certain body parts and, in the days before marketers and focus groups, people often called them as they saw them rather than as they might appeal to consumers. You don't have to be Sigmund Freud to see peppers as phallic symbols. So it's not surprising that, in many cultures, peppers are called penises. In Swahili, chili peppers are *pili-pili*, which is slang for penis. And a variety of hot red chili pepper is called peter pepper or penis pepper.

Similarly, the Aztecs thought avocados were shaped like testicles, so that's what they called them: *ahuacatl*. The Spanish adapted it to *aguacate*; in English, it is avocado. Avocados were also thought to be aphrodisiacs, again probably because of their shape.

Sicilians thought small eggplants looked like testicles, and named a stuffed baby eggplant dish *Cugghiune dell' Ortolano*, according to Clifford Wright's *Cucina Paradiso*. The phrase translates to Farmhand's Balls.

Our menu included three desserts, but we might have had many more. Virgin's Breasts, or *Minni di Virgini*, are puffy, round pastries that are filled with preserves or *biancomangiare* (a custard) and then baked. Mary Taylor Simeti, author of *Pomp and Sustenance*, says that in Catania, Sicily, a similar pastry is topped with a cherry and called *Minni di Sant'Agata*, or Saint Agatha's Breasts, in tribute to the martyr who is usually pictured holding her severed breasts on a plate.

The breast theme may continue with the cheese course. In Spain, a mild cow's milk cheese molded into the rounded shape of a breast culminating in a nipple is known as a *tetilla*. Although *tetilla* does translate to nipple, it actually means a male nipple according to my dictionary. The shape of the cheese is distinctly female. It is supposed to have originated in Santiago de Compostela. According to travel writer Shirley

Moskow, the portico of the town's cathedral once featured a voluptuous carving of Queen Esther next to an admiring statue of Daniel. The church fathers were so dismayed they had a sculptor give her a breast reduction. Local cheese makers retaliated by shaping their cheeses as buxom breasts and displaying them all over town.

Buttocks are almost as popular as breasts on the dining table. Chancellor's Buttocks, or *Fedde del Cancelliere*, is a Sicilian fried pastry. After frying, the rounded patties are filled with *biancomangiare*, closed, rolled in sugar, and sprinkled with cinnamon. Buttocks Sandwiches, or *Sciatre e Matre*, are their savory counterparts. The dish is made from eggplant slices sandwiched with béchamel sauce and then deep-fried. Clifford Wright says the phrase is a Sicilian euphemism for buttocks.

Our third dessert, Mother-in-Law's Tongues, *Lingue di Suocera* in Italian, are cookies filled with marmalade or jam. They are small and sweet—just what we hope our own mother-in-law's tongue will be. The same term is also used for a long, crisp flat bread, which is shaped more like a tongue.

Milk of our Blessed Mother, the wine we served with dessert, is better known as *Liebfraumilch*, a popular sweet white wine from Germany. Apparently we'd rather try to pronounce *Liebfraumilch* than refer to or think about drinking the Blessed Mother's milk.

It was difficult to settle on just a few desserts because this category has a prodigious number of dishes named for body parts, mostly women's, and frequently with religious associations.

We could have nibbled on the eyes of Saint Lucy, *Occhi di Santa Lucia*, a cookie shaped like eyes and named for the protector of eyesight. Apostle's Fingers, *Diti di Apostoli*, from Puglia, are slender, finger-shaped crepes filled with sweetened and liqueur–laced ricotta. A Portuguese egg pudding is called *Barriga de Friera*, or Nun's Tummy. *Petite Religieuse*, little nun, consists of two choux puffs filled with chocolate, coffee, or vanilla pastry cream. They're placed one on top of another and frosted to resemble a nun in her habit, according to Patricia Wells, writing in *The Food Lover's Guide to France*.

When similar choux puffs are deep-fried, they make a little burst of sound. So the French call them by the charming name *Soupirs de Nonne*, or nun's sighs. They're also known as *Pets de Nonne*, or nun's farts.

Then there are the sweets named after ladies and their fingers, navels, and mouths. *Dame Blanche*, or White Lady, is a French version of a hot fudge sundae. It's also the name of vanilla butter cookies sandwiched together with raspberry jam, with a heart-shape cut out of the top cookie to reveal the red raspberry filling. A White Lady cocktail is made with gin, lemon juice, and an orange liqueur.

Lady's Mouth, *Bocca di Dama*, is a delicate almond sponge cake, traditionally served as a Passover dessert in Italy. Lady's Navel, *Hanim Göbegi*, is a Turkish dessert consisting of round, walnut-size pastry balls with a slight indentation pressed into their middles. They're deep-fried, then soaked in sweet syrup. Bride's Fingers, *Asabia el Aroos*, are a Middle Eastern treat made from slender crisps of phyllo pastry and filled with sweetened nuts.

Of course we can't forget Ladyfingers, the crisp sponge cookies that are also known as boudoir biscuits. They form the base of the Charlotte Russe, a dessert the great French chef Antonin Carême invented. Charlotte's poor relation is a Betty, a dessert that combines fruit and bread crumbs rather than ladyfingers.

Not all desserts turn out perfectly. The British are famed for their puddings, and they're also known for the imaginative names they give puddings that fail. Jane Garmey lists a few supremely unappetizing ones: Boiled Baby, Wet Nelly, Dead Man's Leg, and Washerwoman's Arm.

Our late-night snack of Bones of the Dead and Corpse Revivers is more delectable than it sounds. The bones, *ossi di morte* in Italian, are crisp white cookies, often served on All Souls' Day in remembrance of deceased relatives. The Corpse

Reviver is a cocktail made with almond liqueur, maraschino liqueur, and yellow Chartreuse, poured to form three distinct zones of color, according to William Grimes author of *Straight Up or On The Rocks*. Whether it's strong enough to wake the dead or not, it is a colorful way to end the evening.

—

You may want to recreate this menu exactly or you may prefer to substitute some of the other options I've described. Either way, I'm sure you'll have a memorable meal. So, now that you've entertained the possibilities, why not have some friends for dinner tonight?

FLOUTING THE TABOO

Ellen J. Fried

THE DEPICTION OF CANNIBALISM IN ADVERTISING

Introduction

Cannibalism has been dubbed the last taboo. If that were indeed the case, one would not expect to see cannibalism discussed or depicted much outside of scholarly journals or the occasional sensational newspaper article. Yet just the opposite is true.

Images of cannibalism are everywhere in our culture. It is the subject of jokes and cartoons. It is the topic of movies, both pornographic and for general audiences, books, poems and songs. It is the name of at least one pop singing group, "The Fine Young Cannibals." And the depiction of cannibalism in advertising is also, pun intended, alive and well.

In fact, the use of cannibal images to sell products has been around for more than one hundred years. The stereotypical black cannibal dancing around a boiling cauldron meant to cook whichever hapless white person is available, be it missionary, shipwreck survivor or tourist, has been used to sell items ranging from chewing gum to cigarettes. Even though the style of the ad may have changed, from simple pen and ink drawings to sophisticated television commercials, the story line has, incredibly, stayed the same.

As the culture has become more permissive, so has the content of the advertisements. What was once considered obscene has become commonplace. One method employed by advertisers to capture attention is the use of shocking images. Accordingly, the depiction of cannibalism in some advertising has striven to gain attention by presenting what many cultures would consider offensive. For example, one does not expect a surgeon to be armed with napkin, knife and fork at an operation, yet someone at an ad agency thought that image would help boost vodka sales.

The type of products advertised using cannibal images is continually increasing; they include digestive aids, restaurants, chutney and frequent flyer miles. The only aspect of cannibalism that remains taboo, and illegal, is actually doing it, although a very clever website would have the gullible believe that ordering and eating human meat is only a mouse-click away.

Cannibalism may be taboo; the depiction of it in advertising is certainly not. It may be offensive to some. It is definitely funny to many others. Sometimes it's in bad taste. (The puns are inevitable and endless.) What follows are descriptions, discussions and illustrations of advertisements depicting cannibalism. Each reader will have to judge for him- or herself whether the advertising hits the mark.

Historical Basis

Although often described as unthinkable and unmentionable, there is considerable literature that chronicles the history of cannibalism. Reports of ritualistic cannibalism were brought back to Europe by Spanish conquistadors. South Pacific travelers also told tales of island tribes that ceremonially cooked and ate their enemies in some rituals and their dead relatives in others. Fairy tales and gothic literature are full of cannibalistic imagery.

When did the subject of cannibalism become the fodder for humor? And when did advertisers decide that it was humor that would delight the public sufficiently to draw attention to its products? A simple answer to the former question is that humans tend to laugh at things that frighten them in an effort to relieve their fears. Advertisers will play on many emotions to sell products; humor is certainly employed often in ad copy and commercials.

Flesh and Blood, by Reay Tannahill, a sociological history of cannibalism in Western society, first appeared in 1975. In the preface to the updated 1996 edition, the author mused about prevailing attitudes when the first edition was published:

> *It is easy, now to forget what sensitive stomachs people had in those days; days when the academic index still hid cannibalism under anthropophagy, or endophagy, or exophagy, and Roget's Thesaurus tried to lose it altogether by listing the deed under 'Killing' and the cannibal-as-consumer under 'Food' (positioned, according to some inscrutable logic, between 'carnivore' and 'vegetarian').*

Tannahill theorizes that the social revolutions of the 1960s resulted in the younger generation's desire to shock their elders, while at the same time, loosening sexual mores made it more difficult for the simple depiction of sex to be shocking:

> *Terms and practices that had been largely unknown to genteel grownups a decade before became widely current only with Alex Comfort's 1972 bestseller* The Joy of Sex *(subtitled, with no doubt unintentional timeliness,* A Gourmet Guide to Lovemaking*).*

Since the open discussion of sex was no longer shocking, more deeply ingrained taboos, such as cannibalism, had to be invoked for rebellious youth, or advertisers, to gain the public's attention.

Racial Stereotypes: The Black Savage, Then and Now

The history of blacks in advertising is a topic in its own right. The depiction of blacks as cannibals for advertising purposes has been used for many years. Both South Sea Islanders and Africans were often depicted as ignorant savages in advertisements. Many followed familiar story lines: cannibals' health (mostly indigestion) could be improved if they would eat Western food products or, they could be readily distracted from the business at hand, that is, cooking and eating whites, by culinary treats such as chewing gum.

Promotion for a Lecture

The cannibalistic practices of South Sea Islanders were well known in the 1800s. During the latter half of the century, Mark Twain traveled the country as a lecturer; one such event was a presentation about the Sandwich Islands. The following publicity advertisement, which broadly referred to cannibalism, appeared in newspapers in the Midwest

> *In order to Illustrate the customs of the cannibals of the Sandwich Islands, the lecturer will DEVOUR A CHILD, In presence of the audience, if some lady will kindly volunteer an infant for the occasion.*

Grape-Nuts Cereal

An advertisement for Grape-Nuts Cereal appeared in the Boston Globe on January 22, 1902. The drawing depicted a cannibal with exaggerated lips, leaning against a tree. A cauldron bubbles over hot coals and human skulls and bones are scattered nearby. The caption reads "Good Things in a Bad Place," a reference to tropic locales, and promises that a bowl of Grape-Nuts breakfast food with some rich cream "...will agree with the weakest stomach, and supply the highest form of nourishment, pre-digested and ready for quick change into good, rich blood." If one indulged in eating missionaries however, Grape-Nuts would not help. The copy reads, "Pies, puddings cake and goodies of all sort (missionaries excepted), are intended for human use, but such good things should not be put in a bad stomach..."

Signs and Drainpipe Cleaner

Racism and derogatory references to blacks were commonplace in early advertising. African cannibalism was often the focal point of advertisements with racist overtones in the 1930s.

African tailors constantly measured whites for the stew pot that brewed over roaring flames. One advertisement that served as a calling card for the Scioto Sign Company during the 1930s shows white males sitting in a huge pot of hot steaming water while an African male, complete with bone through his hair, looks at them the way one looks at Sunday dinner; the caption read: "If you don't know that you are over your head by now, you need help." Another advertisement in 1938 for Cannibal, a drainpipe cleaner manufactured by the John Sunshine Chemical Company of Chicago, featured a black male captioned with the slogan, "Eats Everything in the Pipe."

Typical of the period between the turn of the century and the 1930s this African connection was a not-so-subliminal threat to whites, a connection that stirred up subconscious anxieties of black retaliation.

Chewing Gum

In 1933 Beech-Nut also used the stereotypical black cannibal to sell gum. A comic strip style print ad tells the story of shipwrecked whites who are about to become dinner when fast thinking saves the day. Bobby, the young hero, dazzles and distracts the natives with a trick he "won" by redeeming BeechNut candy wrappers. The king is as so amused that he appoints Bobby court magician; the gum also cures the king's indigestion (the cause of the king's sour stomach is left to our imaginations).

The idea that savages could be tricked out of eating hapless whites seems terribly dated. Or does it? Some advertisers think the story line is neither too tired nor politically incorrect. Others modernize their copy by adding sexually provocative details that would not have been appropriate in the 1930s. Perhaps the cannibal image has become so clichéd that it has crossed the line into being "camp." In any event, recent advertisements demonstrate that the black cannibal has not disappeared.

Trading Cards

Trading cards packaged with bubble gum have been collectible items for many years. The Fleer Corporation "Crazy Label" series parodied many familiar brands; the familiar Campbell's soup can is transformed into "Cannibal's" brand "Jungle Soup" made with real people. The family style soup pictures a large cauldron with a white arm and leg flailing above the boiling liquid; a caption reads simply: "Help!" Only the natives are missing.

Pizza

A contemporary television commercial, created in India for Domino's Pizza, opens with a shot of a scantily clad white woman tied to a stake over a steaming cauldron, surrounded by black natives. Suddenly the Domino's delivery boy comes swinging through the vines with boxes of pizza. The cannibals are next shown in close-up, with bones through their noses, hungrily devouring the pizza. The girl is dumped on the ground and forgotten.

Snackfood

A television commercial aired in Peru in the late 1990s, touting Nabisco snack food. A group of natives with bones in their noses dance around whites tied to stakes. The blacks give up the idea of eating the humans when they are given Nabisco treats.

Tourism

Food isn't the only topic of ads that center upon the image of the black cannibal. In 1995, the Norwegian airline Braathens SAFE placed a newspaper advertisement intended to promote the use of frequent flier points on British Airways. The ad showed three black tribesmen holding spears, staring at two tourists. One tourist says: "When they told me that they hadn't seen a white person in more than 10 years, but still remembered the taste, I knew we were in trouble." The ad was pulled when it was decried as racist; a spokesman for the airline commented only that the advertisement was supposed to be amusing.

Cannibal Chutney

The promotion of tourism was purportedly the rationale behind the creation of "Cannibal Chutney" by a team of scientists in the Fiji Islands. The recipe is based on a vegetable relish traditionally eaten during cannibal feasts. The chutney was designed for the "novelty gift" category; an addition meant to help Fiji compete in the international travel market.

As sensitivity to racism grew, the concept of depicting cannibalism in advertisements remained, but in many instances, the skin color of the cannibals changed. Cannibalism was still used to draw attention to products; most frequently, the advertisers intended to be humorous. At other times, the intent is to grab the consumers' interest by use of a shocking image or idea. Savage natives may be in short supply, but cannibals and cannibalism are alive and well in the world of advertising.

More Trading Cards

Eclipse Enterprises of Forestville, California, marketed True Crime trading cards in the 1990s in packets of 12 for $1. The Jeffrey Dahmer card describes his crimes and informs the collector that Dahmer pled guilty to cannibalism (among other things.)

Cigarettes

Joe Camel was retired when it was shown that children, by the age of six, recognized Joe as often as they recognized Mickey Mouse. The replacement campaign, "Mighty Tasty," appeared in magazines as diverse as *People* and *Rolling Stone*. Each ad displayed a provocative picture with irreverent copy.

One ad depicted cave women/natives preparing a man stew; a cigarette dangles from the lips of one of the men in the boiling cauldron. The women hold them captive and prepare more vegetables. The copy reads:

> *Viewer discretion advised:*
> *This ad contains:*
> *HW—Hungry Women*
> *HG—Hot Guys*
> *MS—Man Stew*
> MIGHTY TASTY!

Hiking Boots

The HiTec boot company ran a print ad in 1995 depicting a series of boots. The three sets of boots decreased in number from nine to six to three. The ad copy reads:

> *When you're hiking with friends,*
> *Backpacking with friends,*
> *Or forced to eat your friends*

An article in *Adweek* jokingly gave it the week's award for Best Cannibalism Joke in an Ad. The article continued:

> *Body Copy (and we use that term advisedly) lets retailers know the company has Boots 'for everyone from the novice, to the expert, to the, uh, gourmet.' Funny ad. But if the agency ever invites you to a Donner Party commemorative bash, you might*

want to grab a sandwich before going—and skip the hors d'oeurvres once you're there.

Vodka

Smirnoff Vodka ran an advertising campaign titled "through the bottle;" the theme used a seemingly commonplace photograph that would reveal an extraordinary scene when viewed through the clear vodka bottle. In 1996, Smirnoff ran a Christmas ad campaign that was described as follows:

> *The ad depicts a number of green-gowned surgeons in the middle of a messy operation. One doctor holds a bloody swab while another manipulates a pair of calipers. Through the bottle, a sinister-looking surgeon, holding a knife and fork and with a napkin tucked into his operating gown, stares out.*
>
> *A spokesman for the ad agency described the campaign by explaining that: "These executions [pun intended?] are more consciously polarizing. Some people will love them, others won't." So true, but will they sell more vodka?*

Alka-Seltzer

This is an updated version of the necessity for a digestive after eating human meat, especially if you haven't any BeechNut gum handy. In 1997, Alka-Selzer ran a television ad in the UK that began with the image of two shipwrecked men in a lifeboat, which then faded to one man. The voice-over intoned: "Alka-Seltzer—when you've eaten something you shouldn't have."

According on one newspaper report, the ad was pulled when forty viewers complained to the Independent Television Commission, a watchdog group. A spokesman explained that the majority of complainants objected to the allusion to cannibalism and, as such, was in bad taste. He further stated that; "Some people think cannibalism to be a taboo subject for advertising, and this ad was considered to be offensive by some viewers. The number of complaints we received over it is more than we would normally get, so obviously it touched a raw nerve with some people."

Bayer, the maker of Alka-Seltzer, refused to comment for the article. They have more recently failed to respond to an e-mail I sent seeking information about the commercial.

Blue Jeans & Other Clothing

A French company, Blink jeans, used the shock value of a photograph depicting human body parts wrapped in typical supermarket style to advertise their jeans. The pictures have nothing to do with jeans; presumably, the brand of jeans will be remembered because of the images in the ad. It is interesting to note that a survey conducted by a New York ad agency found that a large segment of the public finds Calvin Klein and Jordache jeans ads objectionable. Perhaps the French jeans company is just following in this tradition.

The depiction of happy babies is a common advertising theme. Benneton decided to employ the image of black and white babies embracing... in a large stockpot. No copy accompanied the ad; Benneton apparently felt that the picture said it all. Exactly what is being said, however, remains elusive.

Restaurants

Esquire magazine featured an article in February 2001 entitled "Stick a fork in him, he's done." The chef of Blue Hill Restaurant in New York City was interviewed for his thoughts on "people preparation;" he describes the most desirable victim as, "reasonably healthy but with a little paunch for flavoring," details selected cooking methods and advises that, "Should anyone pop into the kitchen and realize what you're doing, kill him." The article is illustrated with a diagram of a human body partitioned into select cuts of meat.

Assorted Merchandise & Politics

The web site www.ManBeef.com was a unique shopping destination; it claims to sell human meat in a politically correct manner. The site was extremely detailed and offered a menu typical of other, more conventional websites such as policies, tips & info, FAQs, recipes and products. ManBeef offered a large selection of merchandise emblazoned with various ManBeef logos including mouse pads, mugs, T-shirts and baseball caps.

Although any attempt to place an order for a human beef product was be unsuccessful, sales of other merchandise has been brisk.

The site elicited the full gamut of emotions from bemusement to revulsion. The site's creator, who calls himself Joseph Christopherson, admits that it was a hoax and opined that it is more difficult to get a rise out of people as society become more jaded and that "The subject of human meat was chosen because of its ability to churn the viewer's stomach and help outrage the more 'sensitive' viewers." Perhaps all of the gory detail was provided to draw attention to the animal rights' agenda. Whatever the motivation, the site garnered a lot of attention.

Conclusion

Cannibalism has been denounced, studied, parodied, laughed at, decried as mere myth and depicted in books, movies and paintings. Advertisers have taken advantage of the topic's ability to, if not sell a product, at least call attention to it. Bon Appetit!

THE HUMAN REMEDY
Janet Clarkson

There are no parts of the body, or its secretions and excretions, which have not sometime, somewhere, been used therapeutically—including feces, menstrual blood, semen, earwax, fat, hair and nails. We have been internally recycling body parts and body fluids for medical purposes for at least as long as we have been recording our history, but without—until very recently perhaps—considering it in any way related to that nasty culinary habit of savage races, which we call cannibalism. The only difference between "then" and "now," as always—is in the details.

One of the earliest known medical treatises is the "Ebers Papyrus," which dates from about 1550 BCE, and contains 700 or so remedies for a wide range of conditions. It demonstrates the high degree of sophistication achieved by the healers of ancient Egypt, and that the use of human body parts for medicine was already well established. Among the ingredients listed in the remedies are human brain (for eye complaints), human dung (in poultices for skin lesions), and semen (for internal use for an "abdominal obstruction").

The other highly developed skill in ancient Egypt of course was the art of embalming, and it is ironic that mummified flesh (ideally sourced from a genuine Egyptian mummy) would become the "snake oil" of Europe three thousand years later. The belief that *"mummy"* or *"mumia"* had healing power was based on a historic riddle wrapped in a linguistic mystery inside a medical enigma. There was a bitumen-like substance called in Arabic *"mumiya"* (or perhaps it was a wax like substance from Persia called *mum*) which oozed from the ground in mountainous areas, and which supposedly had medicinal qualities. Long after the original knowledge had been lost, Europeans came to believe that the Egyptians had used bitumen to embalm bodies, hence these themselves became "mummies," and the healing powers of the mineral went with them. The clear intention of the Egyptians in preserving the flesh to ensure survival in the afterlife surely added its own suggestive power to the formula.

Using parts of man to remedy the diseases of man was perfectly obvious to medieval healers. The received wisdom which had underpinned their philosophy for two millennia, and which it was heretical to challenge, was the ancient Greek doctrine of the humors—a comprehensive holistic view of the natural world, of which man was a microcosm. In medical terms this meant that disease was due to imbalance between the four bodily humors, and the role of healers was to correct these imbalances. The newer Renaissance "doctrine of signatures" (actually old herbal lore rediscovered) and the concept of "sympathetic medicine," or "like cures like" made gradual inroads, but were also perfectly compatible with the use of human flesh and fluids for medicinal purposes.

By the seventeenth century experimental science was in the ascendant, and after the formation of The Royal Society in 1660, it never looked back. Nevertheless, old ideas die hard, particularly where anxieties run high such as in matters of life and health, and human and animal flesh and excretions continued to be used for a century or so after they were removed from the London Pharmacopoeia in 1747.

There were three products called "mummy" or "mummia:" mummified flesh, of a *"strong but disagreeable smell,"* the rarer dark, viscous liquid which oozed from the bodies during embalming process with a *"not disagreeable smell;"* and the original mineral "Jew's Pitch." The first was the most common, but prescribers would sometimes clarify which preparation they intended.

The demand for mummified flesh was so great in the sixteenth and seventeenth centuries that, even though a huge grave-robbing industry and international trade in mummies had developed, it could not always be filled. Entrepreneurs have never been in short supply however, and a trade in fakes grew up, the demand being met by the quick bitumenizing and drying of any available body, however obtained. Eventually there was further disconnection from the original medicinal product, and flesh and bones from unmummified corpses were used.

Often the mummified flesh was simply pulverized before being hung around the neck as an amulet against the plague, or mixed with other ingredients in an unguent or medicine. Sometimes it was pre-prepared in some way, such as in this "elixir" from *"The Art of Distillation"* (1651), by the alchemist John French.

> *Elixir of Mummy is made thus*
>
> *Take of mummy (viz., of man's flesh hardened), cut small four ounces, spirit of wine terebinthinated ten ounces, and put them into a glazed vessel (three parts of four being empty) which set in horse dung to digest for the space of a month. Then take it out and express it, and let the expression be circulated a month. Then let it run through manica hippocratis, and then evaporate the spirit until that which remains in the bottom be like an oil which is the true elixir of mummy.*
>
> *This elixir is a wonderful preservative against all infections, also very balsamical.*

Recipes for mummy and other body parts frequently specified that the flesh be obtained from one who had died a violent death, which again made perfect sense at the time. We have always liked some magic with our medicine (which is fortunate for we still need the placebo effect), and the occult or spiritual power of the medicine was more powerful if the death had been sudden or violent, for the cause of death was identifiable and the life force not ebbed away but "captured" in the flesh. Executed criminals were the most acceptable source of body parts, their punishment then being eternal, as it was believed that the desecration of the body would prevent resurrection on judgment day—so not something to be done to the body of a good Christian.

Naturally, the "vital spirit" was even stronger if the body was from a young, "lusty" or "unblemished" man. The alchemist Oswald Croll actually specified the age of 24 years, and he also preferred the corpse from a red-headed man. The color red, the color of blood itself, has always wielded a special power in medicine. Red cloths were wrapped around arthritic joints and hung in the rooms of smallpox sufferers, and the color of stimulant remedies enhanced with red herbs and stones. A remedy for a "plaister" for a rupture of the *"Testicles and Cods"* from a medical text of 1598 specifies as an ingredient *"the bloud of a red bearded and healthfull man."* Before we scoff, we should note that we are still suggestible in this way—modern studies have shown that people given placebos perceive red capsules to have a more "stimulating" effect than blue or green.

What better solution for the serious things that ailed you than "essence of man" himself?

Mumia was usually reserved for the most frightening or life-threatening conditions, when this "essence" was most at risk. That it was one of the most exotic, imported, and expensive remedies available would surely, as happens today, have added to its "power."

The battlefield provided plenty of opportunities for its use. Oswald Gabelkover in his *Boock of Physicke* (1599) used it in medicines *"for all woundinge,"* in any man who had been *"thruste, Shotte, or els hath fallen."* It could be given with confidence, for *"when you administer the same to anye bodye which is halfe deade ... he shall be agayne revivede."*

Variations of the remedies were for *"congleled blood"* (dangerous, because it represented an excess of that humor), and the *"gangrenation"*—surely a terrifying condition in any era? —after which *"you shall behoulde miracles."*

Childbirth was the potentially fatal battlefield for women, and Gabelkover used mummy "neat" in his remedy for a very sinister obstetric situation.

> *For difficult parturione, or Childbirthe*
>
> *When a woman hath noe travayle*
>
> *Give unto her Mummye, the quantitye of a Pease, with wine to drincke."*

If the woman could not be delivered of a *"deade Childe"* he recommended:

> Take Mummye, *Viscus quersinus [mistletoe of the oak], white Ambre [amber], & the spermaticks of a Hinde [from the genitals of a deer] of each the biggenes of a pease contunde it smalle & give it to her to drincke ether with wine, or Lillywater.*

Mummy powder was used externally too. Dr. William Salmon *"one of his majesties Physicians in Ordinary"* used it for post-natal *"falling down of the fundament."* It was mixed with human breast milk and herbs, dried to powder, and strewn upon the prolapsed womb, which was then *"put up as aforesaid."*

Aside from its use in injuries and childbirth, mummy was included in remedies for wasted limbs, consumptions, "fluxes and rheums," apoplexy, "pestilence and dropsey," "joints that are out of place," "flux of the semen and night pollutions," the "falling sickness" and even nosebleeds. There were only a few dissenting voices: one physician called it a "wicked kinde of drugge" that caused "a stinke of the mouth," to another it was an "unnatural and horrid physick," but for most it was an effective panacea.

What to do when the expensive import is not available as a panacea? Find a more accessible one of course—human bone, especially skull bone.

Robert Boyle, eminent scientist, and leading light of the new Royal Academy suffered from chronic ill health, or at least chronic anxiety about his health, and used "skull moss" as a remedy for his own nosebleeds. The moss that grew on human skulls had a reputation for healing since very early medieval times. It was believed that it had absorbed the "virtue" or life force from the body—in the same way that mandrakes growing beneath the gallows fed on the semen ejaculated from the dying hanged man—and thus became acceptable substitutes for the corpse itself. Actual skull bone was perhaps even better than mere moss. Like mummy, it could be ground up and used "neat," or made into an elixir or tincture. John French included a formula for *"A Famous Spirit made out of Cranium Humanum"* in his text, which he mentions was similar to Dr. Goddard's famous "Spirit of Skulls." He says that the spirit *"helps the falling sickness, gout, dropsie, infirm stomach, and indeed strengthens all weak parts, and opens all obstructions, and is a kind of panacea."* Dr. Goddard (who was accused by some of his detractors of substituting hartshorn for the real thing) reputedly sold the formula to King Charles II, who reputedly prepared it himself, and partook of it in his final illness—not a good endorsement, as by all accounts he had an unpleasant dying, surrounded by physicians who were satisfied that "nothing was left untried."

The "Eminently Learned" Sir Kenelm Digbie, a colorful and eccentric founding member of the Royal Society, like Boyle did not let the absence of a medical degree stop him publishing a book of medicines. In *"Choice and experimented receipts in physick and chirurgery"* he used skull bone in a remedy for heavy menstrual bleeding (coyly titled in Latin, as "sensitive" medical problems often were).

> *Remedium ad Fluxum immoderatum Sanguinis Menstrualis.*
>
> *Take the Scull of a man, scrape of it one dram, put it into a glass of White-wine, let it infuse a night, and in the morning take it fasting. In two or three times taking it every two days, it will cure it.*

Gabelkover kept his formula simple in his remedy for burns due to gunpowder. Presumably the wounded soldier would have preferred the version containing beer.

> *Extinction of the Gunnepouder.*
>
> *Take rasped bone of the Forehead of a deade mans sculle, & let the Patiente drincke the same with Beer, or with water, & it will immediately helpe.*

The most common and enduring use of skull bone however, over many centuries, was for "the falling sickness" (epilepsy), a mysterious and frightening ailment that early physicians recognized as originating in the head—the obvious rationale for using bone from the head in a remedy. Again, bone from an executed man was preferable, even if the patient was a child. This remedy from *Practice Medicinae* (1598), which had eight pages on the topic, was presumably for the child of a rich family, as it contained genuine pearls and gold, sweetened as we would nowadays, to make the medicine go down:

> *Of the Falling sicknesse in children.*
>
> *A Powder*
>
> *Take halfe a drag. of the scull of an executed man, prepared Pearles one drag. Harts horne two scrup. Tormentil, Seduarie, of each two scrup. Sugar candie one ounce and a halfe, five leaves of beaten gold; temper them all togither, and give it to the sicke body with Pionie water and such like.*

An alternative pediatric remedy in the same book was a simple *"water of Cow dung... half an ounce at least,"* perhaps for the poorer patients.

Each of the experts, of course, added their own variations to the basic skull bone formula.

Nicolas Culpeper (quoting Paracelsus) specified the exact part of the skull—"that small triangular bone in the Skul of a man, called Os triquetrum, so absolutely cures the falling-sickness that it will never come again." Digby added herbs, mistletoe (which never "falls down" from the treetops) and "Parings of Nails of Man." Salmon (whose medical degree did not stop him including culinary recipes) wrote a "Family dictionary, or, Household companion" (1695) in which the topics were arranged in alphabetical order (so Gammon of Bacon comes immediately before Gangreen), and his formula included rasping of elks-hoof and nutmeg. John Shirley in "The Accomplished Ladies Rich Closet of Rarities" (1691) also included nutmeg, which in this case may have helped disguise the inclusion also of canine blood.

> *An Excellent Powder for the Falling-Sickness.*
>
> *Take a Mans Scull that has not been above a year buried ...bury it in hot embers ... beat it into a powder; then grate a Nutmeg, and put it to it, with two ounces of the Blood of a Dog dried and powdered. Mingle them together, and give the grieved party a dram Morning and Evening in White-wine or new Milk.*

Other bone was also useful. Robert Boyle sensed no dissonance with either his devout religious faith or his passionate belief in experimental science when he included the following formula in *"Medicinal Experiments, or, A Collection of Choice and Safe Remedies ..."*

> *An Uncommon, but Experience'd Remedy for Dysenterical Fluxes.*
>
> *Take the Bone of the Thigh of a hang'd Man (perhaps another may serve, but this was still made use of). Calcine it to whiteness, and having purg'd the Patient wth an Antimonial Medicine, give him one Dram of this white Pouder for one Dose, in some good Cordial, whether Conserve or Liquor.*

Of course, if skull moss is good, and skull bone is better, perhaps brain tissue itself is best? There were certainly recipes for the essence or spirit of human brains—again, preferably from *"a young man that has died a violent death"*—but evidence for the actual use or prescription of this essence, or any other preparation of brain tissue, is uncommon by the seventeenth century. Perhaps even the seventeenth century patient was too squeamish.

Something similar seems to have applied to the use of human blood as a remedy. Many of the references are myth-tory rather than history—tales of aristocrats bathing in or drinking the blood of specially procured children to preserve their beauty, as in the stories of sixteenth century countess Elizabeth Bathory, or Louis XI (to cure his supposed leprosy) or Pope Innocent VIII (when he was near death).

Since ancient times there has been a sense of something repulsive or sinister about the direct ingestion of fresh hot blood, some feeling that it is non-human. In Roman times, it was the treatment for epilepsy. Pliny reports it *"Naturalis Historia"* but clearly finds it bestial and disgusting:

> *Epileptic patients are in the habit of drinking the blood even of gladiators, draughts teeming with life, as it were; a thing that, when we see it done by the wild beasts even, upon the same arena, inspires us with horror at the spectacle! And yet these persons, forsooth, consider it a most effectual cure for their*

> *disease, to quaff the warm, breathing, blood from man himself, and, as they apply their mouth to the wound, to draw forth his very life; and this, though it is regarded as an act of impiety to apply the human lips to the wound even of a wild beast!*

Nevertheless, well before knowledge of its circulation, blood was associated with the very essence of life itself. How then to capture and use this "essence," but avoid the associations with beasts, pagans, savages, or practitioners of the dark arts? Mummy and skull bone were processed beyond recognition by the time they reached most end-users (to blackish or whitish powders respectively). It would make sense to do the same with blood. Powder of blood was applied to wounds and "ruptures," and blood was also distilled to a spirit or "elixir" which had keeping qualities and would not have looked so "bloody."

There was no shortage of human blood for use in remedies—blood-letting was a common therapeutic technique for three thousand years—but sometimes an alternative was given, as in this remedy from 1569.

> *To heale the trembling or shaking of the members.*
>
> *Anoynt the crowne of the heade and the places that are grieved with oyle of Cinnamonde, and cause the diseased person to take two drammes of the water that is made of mans or Swines bloud, brought into putrefaction with Aqua vitæ, and after distilled, and of this you must give him to drinke many times in a Moneth.*

As with all other body tissues, not all blood was believed to be equal. As we have seen, according to one writer the blood of a healthy red-headed man was of particular value, for another the best quintessence of blood was made from that of *"good natured or angry young men who drink good wines."* Menstrual blood has always been in a different category.

In ancient cultures menstrual blood was either sacred or unclean, but always mysterious and magical, being associated with the lunar cycle, and with connotations of primitive female power and pagan fertility rites. In spite of its occult power there are few actual written remedies that use it as an ingredient. Perhaps this is because of its association with witches—often old women—whose power and wisdom resided in their retained menses, and who used menstrual blood in spells. Perhaps by its nature it remained predominantly in the armamentarium of female healers and midwives, who did not write the books. There are some references to its use in a variety of complaints—for internal use in the stone and epilepsy, and as an application for gout for example, but little that is specific. Naturally though, it would be expected to have some effect in female problems, and Gabelkover does have a recipe using menstrual blood (*"termes"*) for excessive bleeding in childbirth

> *Agaynst the fluxione of the Cordialle, or Hartebloode, & we feare least the woman should dye therof.*
>
> *Give her then to drincke three droppes of her owne tearmes with a little Hennesbroth.*

It is hardly surprising that the trials and tribulations of childbirth have attracted their share of ritual, and eating the placenta (usually by the mother, as a tonic) has figured large in traditional and folk medicine in many cultures around the world. It is a popular restorative and panacea in China in the form of an extract or pill, with one newspaper report in 1995 also suggesting that there is a thriving market for the large number of aborted fetuses (preferably first-born males from young women) produced as a result of the one-child policy. Eating the placenta has recently become fashionable—in some circles at least—in the West, but this seems to be intended as a "bonding experience" rather than a nutritional or medical one.

The function of the placenta and umbilical cord (the *"secondes"*) was a mystery to medieval practitioners, but its connection with the birth process made it logical that it would be used in relation to problems in that area. Salmon uses the umbilical cord in a remedy for infertility. Again, the first-born boy has the extra power.

> *An Excellent Potion for to cause Conception.*

> *Take the navill-string of a boy that is first-born, which has not touched the ground, being well dryed, beat it to powder, and drink it in Wine.*

It was inevitable that the "secondes" would be tried in the falling sickness. Gabelkover also used the placenta of a male child.

> *Another which is verye certayne.*
>
> *Take of the Secondes, of a Woman, which is deliverede of a man Childe, drye it, & poulder it, & when this disease approchethe anye man we must administer [doses given] either in wyne, or water of blacke Cherryes.*

Human fat is much less complicated than menstrual blood and placenta. It is after all, only *"Mans Grease"* and with very little preparation was useful in ointments for skin and joint problems. It was a perquisite of the executioner in Paris, who sold it unprocessed, unlike the physicians and apothecaries, who value-added with herbs. Gabelkover has a recipe for cancer of the breasts, to be applied after the cancer has been cut and burnt.

> *Of the Cancer of the Breasts*
>
> *Take Herb Robert, Verbascum, or Moulin, Scabious, Caprifolium, or Honey-suckles, Dill, Mans grease, each equal parts; burn them, take three ounces, and with six ounces of Nightshade water in a Leaden Mortar mix them.*

Is the application of body fat to another's skin, strictly speaking, cannibalism? We now know that many medicinal substances are "ingested" by absorption across body membranes—and we take advantage of this in such products as asthma puffers, hormone patches, and angina sprays. Does cannibalism only refer to ingesting by mouth?

What about body fluids and excreta? Does cannibalism only refer to actual flesh?

There is no doubt that healers of all persuasions have clearly intended to transmit the "essence" or vital characteristics of the person from whom these materials have been obtained, so it is not a nutritional or pharmacological issue but a spiritual one, as in acts of ritual cannibalism.

Mother's milk is intended as a food, so perhaps it is not cannibalistic to ingest it. What if the recipient is not a breast-dependent infant, but an adult, and the intent is medicinal? The non-nutritional, remedial use of breast milk is an interesting example of the intention to transmit a specific non-physical quality. It was believed that breast milk was different for male and female children, and remedies often specified which was to be used. In *Practice Medicinae* there is a remedy *"For to bring the sicke to sleepe and rest"* which specifies *"Take womans milke, of one that giveth sucke to a daughter... ."* What female characteristic was being transmitted here?

What is also intriguing is the specifically male conditions for which mother's milk was recommended. Gabelkover recommends it for impotence (using the Latin name again for a "sensitive" topic)

> *Contra Impotentiam, & Incantationes.*
>
> *Take Womans milcke, an rennishe wine glassful, drincke it, & the lost senses will return agayne.*

In "Sixe hundred foure score and odde experienced medicines..." (1569) it is recommended "To remedie the burning of urine" in a male patient. Several ingredients are added to "the white of a new layde Egge" and "the milke of a woman which hath brought forth a daughter." The resulting solution was then "squirted therof into the pipe of the mans member."

A presumably more popular method of administration of mother's milk was directly from the breast—and the recorded recipients, funnily enough, seem to be wealthy old males! In Thomas Cogan's *"Haven of Health"* (1584) he relates the story of the Earl of Cumberland

> *...being brought to utter weakness by a consuming fever, by meanes of a Womans sucke together with the good counsaile of learned Physicians, so recovered his strength, that before being destitute of heires male of his owne bodie, he gate [begot] that*

> *most worthie gentleman that nowe is inheritour both of his fathers vertues and honour [i.e his son].*

Breast milk, believed to be derived from menstrual blood, perhaps had some of its powers, and it was natural to assume its value in obstetric problems. A number of remedies suggest that its medicinal power was increased by giving it secretly. Gabelkover suggests in difficult labour: *"give unto her without her knowledge another womans milcke to drincke,"* as does Salmon who says *"Some give to women that cannot be delivered, (unknown to them) Bitches milk or a good draught of a womans milk,"* he then adds a herbal application to the *"secret parts."*

Drinking one's own urine for health reasons has a long history in many cultures, and also seems to be having a resurgence in popularity. In the past a draught of one's own urine was common for "obstructions," gout, dropsy, jaundice, and to ward off the plague. Drinking another's urine today is more likely to be associated with a sexual fetish than a medical indication, but it was not always so. As we would expect, the preferred donor was often specified, and the urine of male children was usually preferable. One of the many remedies for the falling sickness in *"Practice Medicinae"* includes it…

> *Item, Ravens egs, Swallows flesh, Wolfs, Harts, Fore flesh, either boyled or otherwise, the bloud and flesh of a Wesell tempered with the urine of a manchild.*

Salmon also suggests for a difficult labor that the woman *"drink a good draught of her husbands Urine,"* while her feet are in a separate tubs of hot herb-infused wine. It was probably assumed that as one of her husband's body fluids had caused the baby to be in there, then another of his body fluids might drive it out.

In other examples, Pliny reports *"the urine of eunuchs, they say, is highly beneficial as a promoter of fruitfulness in females,"* Markham suggests the urine from a fasting man as an application for gout (probably because gout was associated with rich living), and Gabelkover recommends the urine of *"a Mayde which hath her flowers"* (i.e., is menstruating) as an application for stiff limbs.

Urine from a healthy person is sterile while in the bladder, and although it may pick up some contamination as it is voided this is highly unlikely to be dangerous. The same could hardly be said for feces. The medicinal use of dung from a huge range of animals was extremely common in the past, and the human animal was no exception.

Robert Boyle's huge contribution to the big picture of scientific medical thought seems at odds with the actual remedies he recorded, or more correctly simply repeated. It was sufficient that they were recommended to him *"by the Experience of others, or approv'd by my own."* He included this one.

> *To clear the Eyes, even from Filmes.*
>
> *Take Paracelsus's Zibethum Occidentale (viz, Human Dung) of a good Colour and Consistence, dry it slowly till it be pulverable: Then reduce it to an impalpable Pouder; which is to be blown once, twice, or thrice a day, as occasion shall require into the Patients Eyes.*

Two hundred years before germ theory physicians were free from anxiety about disease transmission from tissue or excrement, but it is difficult to understand how an empiric scientist such as Boyle would believe that blowing any sort of powder into the eyes would clear them.

What is interesting though, is the apparent effort to address the aesthetic issues by assigning a Latin name to the human dung which directly addresses the tricky issue of odor. The name *Zibethum Occidentale* seems to be a concession to the value of a musk-like secretion from the civet cat (*Vivetta cibetha*) to perfumery. Alternatively of course it may simply represent the irresistible need for medical practitioners both to jargonize everything and to disguise some of their more unpalatable remedies.

Human dung was used well into the eighteenth century for many conditions. It is almost impossible today to understand how human feces could continue to be recommended for wound inflammation, tonsillitis, or "pestilential carbuncles," or to agree that *"Oil of human dung is the best remedy in cancerous ulcers."* The herbalist Nicholas Culpeper remained enigmatic on the subject. In his *Physicall directory... A translation of the London dispensatory* (1649) he includes a chapter on medicaments obtained from *"Parts of living creatures and excrements"* but says *"As for the vertues of Excrements, for some reasons (best known to my self) I shall be silent in."*

We must remember that medicine is always "modern" to its practitioners of the day, and our own medicine is tomorrow's old-fashioned. We may feel superior to these old practitioners with their amusing or disgusting or downright sinister remedies, but it behooves us to remember that an awful lot of these body parts and fluids are still used in medicine today.

Microbiology and immunology have made body-part recycling safer, so that transfusions and organ transplants are routine events, but technology has also sanitized the process in a different sort of way too. It has done this by better disguising the origins of some materials, allowing us to maintain our sense of superiority to savage flesh-eating cannibals—if we pause to consider any association at all of course.

You might shudder at the thought of a draught of urine, but would probably willingly welcome an infusion of urokinase—derived from human urine—to dissolve massive blood clots in your lungs. The apothecary may no longer supply powdered thigh bone to treat your dysentery, but the orthopedic surgeon may well use cadaver-derived "demineralized bone matrix" to fill gaps in your own.

And are stem-cells the new mummy? They contain the potential (the "essence" perhaps) to enable them to develop into any human cell, and they may well save our ageing population from modern "plagues" such as Alzheimer's and Parkinson's disease. The current ethical debate about using fetal tissue may even be solved by sourcing them from human fat (a.k.a., "mans greace")—perhaps recycled from someone else's liposuction.

After several millennia with a firm place in the medical armamentarium, the use of body parts was in the doldrums for two centuries, but since the 1950s their use has grown exponentially. We may not use, as Pliny reported the Greeks doing, *"the scrapings from the bodies of athletes,"* and I have been unable to find current medicinal uses for earwax, nail parings, and a few other bits of body debris, but more parts are in current (albeit well-disguised) use than not.

The only significant difference from the old days is that now, usually, we bypass the taste buds.

Shrek, Enfant Terrible and Ex-Cannibal

Darius Willoughby

It took many repeat viewings of the movie *Shrek* with my young sons to fully appreciate the significance of the protagonist's background and his appeal as a pop culture anti-hero. Shrek's historical lineage, as an ogre, is resolutely cannibal. He is the primitive, solitary and uncivilized foil to humans: close to them, but uncouth, unevolved. He is, in a sense, humans' ancestor, the one who chose to remain wild, free of the shackles of modern life and its refined diet of cultivated produce and domestic animals. He is literally the "Other" in the European consciousness, before the Imperialist imagination could project that primitive image onto indigenous peoples of the New World and elsewhere. Shrek comes in many guises, Enkidu in the Gilgamesh epic, Grendel in Beowulf, and as a fee-fie-fo-fumming Giant in much European folklore. In all cases, he is the raw bestial human unfettered by convention and culture. He is also the embodiment of our own fundamental desires. And he gets to eat humans.

In all versions there are two possible endings. Either the ogre is defeated and killed, just as our own urges are stifled, or he is converted, made into one of us. Civilization swallows him up and in a sense cannibalizes the ogre first. Our urges are sublimated into culture. Or at least that is how most versions end. Robinson Crusoe's man Friday is transformed. But Shrek's story is a little different; the conversion process is never quite complete. After all, he remains an ogre, the physical embodiment of the cannibal.

We never actually see Shrek consume human flesh, though he does exploit terrified humans' expectations of his culinary preferences. He tells them how he grinds human bones for his bread, standard ogre fare, and how he sucks the jelly from their eyes. As a cannibal, his tastes are remarkably discriminating and refined. Of course, the stories merely serve to frighten them away so he can enjoy his swamp in peace. And the humans oblige by fleeing. Shrek actually eats many other revolting foods that humans would shun—surprisingly, very methodically with a knife and fork. But the question of whether he has ever really eaten a human, as expected by his reputation is left ambiguous. In the end it is also irrelevant, because from the moment we meet him, he is already in the process of transformation, he has already, unwillingly, taken on a friend in the form of a talking donkey. He is already becoming civilized, and civilized people do not consume their friends. In fact, he has begun to share his food.

This is only the first step toward civil behavior. He is also tamed by the female—much as the wild man in Gilgamesh—and, though he is not offered an inviting display of girlie parts, he does learn to love. Though Princess Fiona, so we think, is a human and Shrek knows very well no human could love an ogre. In the sequel, Shrek and Fiona are even married, and he goes to meet her family, who turn out to be just as bestial—in fact, literally. Fiona's father is a frog, magically transformed into a human king.

Interestingly, Shrek does not in the end become fully human—he has the chance with magic, and briefly does so thinking he will better fit in with Fiona and her family. But as we have learned in part one, Fiona is not fully human either. Every night at sun down (away of course from the leering eyes of civil society, when her primal urges are unleashed) she becomes an ogre. This is the basis of their relationship. Both are semi-civilized, behaving as a happy human couple, but retaining their wild uncouth ogre ways. For example, both belch and fart at the table freely. "Better out than in I always say." His comments suggest that although he has no intention of "behaving" with manners, he nonetheless recognizes that someone—the fully human—would be offended by his actions. They are an odd but happy couple, in touch with their primal urges, living happily in the swamp.

This is all simple enough, but the deeper question, why and how could an ogre become a pop hero, especially for children—for boys to be more specific? There is the obvious identification with a grotesque green monster. Children often see themselves as apart from the rational adult, fully human world. They feel victimized by the expectations of society, not to belch or fart at the table, for instance. Just as Shrek is the primitive human, he is also the child. One who would eat pond muck if he hadn't been told not to, and as I would argue, one who would eat human flesh if given the chance.

That is, we can plot Shrek on a continuum of humanity, just as we can plot children in the process of acculturation. Like the breast-feeding infant, he was first a real cannibal, or so his reputation would suggest. By the time we meet him, or rather by the time children meet him in the movie, he has been weaned. Shrek has moved on to merely repulsive wild foods—though eaten politely, which of course adds to the humor. But he also eats alone. Through the movie we see him gradually change his diet and eat socially. In a memorable scene in part two, he is eating fully human food, although tearing it apart like a beast, as does his father in law (also an animal). By the end Shrek and Fiona resist becoming fully human, just as children could not yet become fully adult. This it seems is the basis for empathy and identification. The heroes can be happy though ugly and ogre (despite what society tells us about being beautiful, thin and polite). Children can be happy too, even though they may not yet fulfill any of society's expectations. They too exist somewhere between the cannibal and the fully human.

Recipes

Dutch Baby

Put your baby in the blender. Puree at high speed. Add a dozen eggs, three cups of flour and a tablespoon of baking soda. Heat a cast iron skillet in the oven at 400 degrees. Drop in a stick of butter and let it melt. Pour all but a tablespoon of your melted butter into the baby batter and mix well. Pour the batter into the pan and add sliced apples. Then put the pan in the oven and let bake for about ten minutes until puffy. Sprinkle with powdered sugar and serve with lingonberry jam on the side.

Ken Albala

Eskimo Ice Cream or Akutag

Choose a juicy ripe Eskimo, or if necessary an old one, which are occasionally found on ice flows. Remove the fat and chop into fine pieces. Add seal oil and a little water. With your hands, whip into a frothy mass. Add salmon berries, and if desired sugar, though this is not traditional. Consume immediately. This can also be sandwiched between two crisp chocolate wafers, for a dandy Eskimo Pie.

Ken Albala

Dingleberry Pie

The best Dingleberry Pies are made from a good variety of berries. Select some from young bushes—they'll be sweeter, but hard to gather since the bushes have such sparse foliage. Berries from older bushes are easier to pick, are more fragrant, and many are blessed with a very desirable "late harvest" quality that lends character to the finished dish. Prepare just as you would a Blueberry Pie—but, unless you are fortunate enough to collect some Tart Dingleberries, you may need to adjust the flavor with a bit of lemon juice.

These pies are generally be made without a "bottom crust," as many connoisseurs feel that it is merely redundant.

Gary Allen

COFFEE & CORDIALS

"I won't eat anything that has intelligent life, but I'd gladly eat a network executive or a politician."
Marty Feldman

GRIMMA GÆST

K. A. Laity

ANGLO-SAXON ENGLAND'S LEGENDARY CANNIBAL

The anonymous (and almost certainly monastic) poet who wrote the Anglo-Saxon epic *Beowulf* centuries ago left many riddles for the curious. We can never know for sure what motivated him to write this epic saga. It may have been nostalgia for his people's pagan past as glorious warriors, or perhaps a desire to insert Christianity into that past, but surely he did not intend to create the first memorable cannibal in English literature. But Grendel, the bone-chomping, blood-drinking descendant of Cain, lives on in nightmarish splendor.

When I teach *Beowulf*, I always begin with an introduction to the warrior ethos of that England long ago, where a stoic faith in *wyrd* (fate) and an overwhelming zeal for fame helped create poems exalting the carnage of the battlefield. According to Old English poetry, a man's worth was determined by his actions in arms. Did he overwhelm his enemies, did he fight for his lord, and did he gain fame for his exploits? Given this harsh warrior code, what kind of monster would be enough to terrify those who dealt daily with death and slaughter?

Grendel terrifies because he turns the warriors' world upside down. He is alone, in contrast to the heroic *comitatus* band. He fights without weapons, invulnerable to their blows. He attacks the mead hall, the social center of life, where mead is drunk, and stories are told of combat survived and deeds remembered. He attacked at night, the "grim ghost," and worst of all, he ate his victims.

Imagine: the warriors in their chain mail on the fields of contention had little choice but to feast their eyes upon the litter of battle. Much of Anglo-Saxon poetry reiterates this image and the expected banqueters, the wolf and the raven, are a commonplace trope. Would a weary combatant ever salivate over the red flesh surrounding him, hungry, despairing, and bone-tired? But taboos are strong. It is an idea too horrible to contemplate—except through the mirror of the anti-warrior, Grendel.

The poet shares the Anglo-Saxon habit of terse language. The understatement of the heroic style focuses more on Grendel's shameful heritage, kin to the first brother-killer, than on his crime. Thirty men he grabbed from the sleeping thanes in Heorot then ran home, "boasting of his booty," to enjoy the feast of slaughter. At first it seems the poet cannot bring himself to dwell on the image. He has it happen off-stage, in Grendel's darkened lair, where no man has ever set foot. He hints at the deeds, but says men may not know the shadowy world where the *helruna* dwells. But this delicacy serves only to whet the appetite, for when he brings hero and monster together his reticence fades.

Beowulf himself brings up the subject with mordant humor, saying there'll be no need to dig him a grave, "as his mouth will cover me well enough." The Geatish warrior knows that he stands the chance of becoming a "bloody feast" when the lonely one eats him. This boldness unlocks the word-hoard of the ancient king, Hrothgar, who is able at last to mourn the horrendous attacks, lamenting the mead hall slick with the blood of the missing men. To prove his worth, Beowulf tells his story of facing nine sea serpents in the ocean. They, too, intended to eat him, gathering around this surprise banquet. Instead it is he who "serves" them a sword feast. Confident in the young warrior, Hrothgar cedes the hall for the night, although one can forgive him for expecting to find only a bloody repast in the morning.

Beowulf lays down with one eye open. Grendel leaves his watery cave and strides toward the mead hall, "not for the first time," as the poet sardonically notes. He burst through the doors, their iron bindings calling to mind the tinge of blood that follows Grendel, the "mouth" of the hall echoing his own gaping maw. His eyes light up at the feast before him, shining out like fire in the darkness in "expectation of the feast." The poet allows the reader to share that moment of salivation, because he even allows Beowulf, the conquering hero, to partake of it as well. Rather than immediately jumping up to grapple with his opponent as he earlier boasted, the warrior watches Grendel feast upon one of his close companions.

Over the years, I have had several students ask, "Why does he just lay there and let his friend get eaten?" I have never arrived at an entirely adequate answer. The common one is that he needs to study how the cannibal moves, the better to fight him. It is less than satisfactory, however; twelve years experience has given Hrothgar and his remaining men a very good idea of how Grendel attacks. Perhaps the hero is shocked into immobility, at least temporarily. One possibility we must consider—however reluctantly many approach the idea—is that the poet does this deliberately to allow the reader to gaze through Beowulf's eyes at the otherwise unspeakable atrocity, the ever-present taboo of warrior life, cannibalism.

The poet makes a spectacle of the death of Hondscio. Grendel snatches his sleeping body (at least he is not conscious of the horror) and literally rips him apart. As Beowulf watches, the fiend bites into the joints of his companion, then slurps the blood from his veins and gobbles up morsels of his flesh. In less time than it takes to tell, he has eaten all of the "unliving" man, including the feet and hands. It happens faster than he can relay it, yet here the poet stretches out the incident in vivid description. This kind of elaboration we come to expect when the poet describes gifts given to triumphant warriors, but not for horrors better left unsaid. Even when Beowulf returns to his Geatish homelands, he emphasizes the horror of his companion's death, how he was completely devoured, eaten up by the "bloody-toothed killer."

Beowulf's retaliation matches Grendel's savagery. With brutal intimacy, the warrior leaps up and pulls Grendel close. The creature pulls away, and in a vicious dance, Beowulf moves with him, gripping his hand so their fingers burst. They wrestle back and forth across Heorot, upsetting mead benches and making the walls resound. Grendel sings his canticle of defeat. Beowulf's win comes not at point of his sword, but with his very fingers. The poet again draws our attention to the flesh, this time to Grendel's. We see through his eyes as Beowulf rips his flesh, first a sore wound tears open his shoulder. The sinews spring open, the tissue bursts apart. The arm comes off in Beowulf's mighty grip and Grendel, terrified and weeping, escapes home to die.

Beowulf stands there, soaked in his foe's blood, a torn limb in his arms. What better revenge than to eat the cannibal who has eaten his friend? The hero lets the moment of triumph sink in, while the poet allows the reader to feel the weight of those twelve bloody years lift. The end of the scene he renders with words both ominous and ambiguous. Ironically, the poet tells us "that was a clear sign" when the hero that hand (arm and shoulder, all that was Grendel's grip) "alegde." The verb is tellingly indefinite despite the assertion of clarity; what does Beowulf do with the hand? Does he fasten it, display it, lay it down or destroy it "under the high roof?" The poet gives us the space to wonder about the fate of that arm. He goes on for many lines, telling how other warriors traced the bloody tracks of Grendel back to his lair, how the lake boiled with blood, how people gathered to celebrate the end of his reign of terror. He even compares Beowulf to the dragon-slaying Sigemund, but it is not until almost one hundred lines later that we are assured the hand of Grendel hangs in the hall on display.

Scholars have generally translated the initial scene of Beowulf alone with the arm in triumph to anticipate that outcome—the bloody trophy flaunted on high. But reading closely, the lines offer us a more ambivalent moment for the hero. Dare he eat the flesh of the defeated kin of Cain? Could he really resist at least tasting the blood of his enemy who, monstrous, invites monstrous behavior? The poet allows us that possibility with his focus on the bloody stump of the arm clutched in the hero's hand like a haunch pulled from a roast. The northern warriors were not above eating raw meat; we have the word of the Viking saga-writers on that. So the bleeding remnant may have been less repugnant to Beowulf than to the modern reader, accustomed to the brand of the grill on her meat.

It leaves us with an uncomfortable realization. If the mighty hero Beowulf—with the strength of thirty men in his arm and the praise of kings ringing in his ears—can be tempted by the lure of torn flesh, who can be free from the fascination? After all, it was Sigemund's son who dared taste the blood of the dragon Fafnir and learned the language of birds. If such secrets lay in a precious drop of red, what further mysteries hide beneath the soft barrier of skin?

THE EYES OF GHOSTS
Mike Lee

PAC-MAN AND CANNIBALISM

Pac-Man, the hero and namesake of the highest capital-producing video game of all time became 25 years old as of June 2005. Was this, perhaps, a cause for celebration? 25 years of video-gaming pleasure, of merchandise (t-shirts, trading cards, lunchboxes, pillow-cases, that marshmallowy breakfast cereal and the divinely sumptuous but now defunct macaroni and cheese); 25 years of sore wrists among the young signifying not the newly-discovered and maniacally-indulged-in joys of autoeroticism but that other delirious pleasure of youth: Pac-Man Fever.

25 years of oodles upon oodles of fun. But also 25 years of hauntings, addiction, and imprisonment in repetitive labyrinths that change only in their increase in danger and nerve-rending intensity. On second thought, it's amazing that Pac-Man's made it to his 25th.

Oh, and one thing I forgot to mention: Pac-Man is a cannibal.

No, no, you might say, don't be silly, he just likes to eat. But the fact is, Pac-Man eats everything. He is the embodiment of pure appetite, a literal pack-man. And if we need evidence of his cannibalistic tendencies, we need look no further than his enemies: the ghosts Inky, Pinky, Blinky and Clyde. Now what possible reason might ghosts have for haunting someone who eats everything he comes into contact with? The dark truth is, the ghosts are the specters of Pac-Man's victims. And the only way Pac-Man can rid himself of them is (through the aid of Super pack pellets) to eat them again. Once eaten, all that remains of the ghosts is their eyes, a fact that could invite any number of theoretical raptures about the "gaze" of the victim—but about which I'll stick to saying that those eyes creep me out how they float back to the center of the labyrinth to re-grow their ghost bodies, and that they serve as a sort of constant reminder that no matter how much Pac-Man eats there's always a remainder that comes back to haunt him. Pac-Man is the original video game antihero, a likeable bad boy who just can't outrun his past.

Okay, so Pac-Man's a cannibal—why should we care? Well, I think we should care because Pac-Man, partly through our culture's addictive relationship with video games (and probably a lot of other stuff too), stands forth as an Everyman. It worries me that nobody seems troubled that the most popular electronic game ever is a game where we get to control this Eater of All Things, where we get to live out the fantasy of inhabiting worlds that exist solely for our consumption. We eat everything and everyone in each level and then move on to the next, eat, move on, and so on, until—what?—well, I've never gotten past the first couple of levels, but my guess is that you eat and repeat until there's nothing and no one left. This, finally, when you've cleared the game, is victory—until, of course the next challenge: Ms. Pac-Man or whatever high resolution, synapse cooking, "world"-clearing game is making worried but exhausted parents limit kids' playtime to three hours per night these days; or, for that matter, another round of good old Pac-Man itself.

But most players don't clear the game; they bite it at Round God-knows-what and pop another quarter in the machine for more pac-fun. Funny that a game about addiction can be so addicting. And, while addictive eating would stand as a pretty solid metaphor for hardcore video-gaming, it's only one side of the coin. The other is solipsism. I mean, these are two of the major criticisms leveled against video games these days, right?—that they're addictive and that they promote antisocial behavior. And, as eminently antisocial or indeed sociopathic as many of the current popular video game fantasies about stealing cars or murdering prostitutes might be, they're only really lame copies on the template of Pac-Man, the supremely asocial video fantasy. If contemporary video game carnage takes place in virtual worlds where cathartic violence replaces the difficulties and complexities of meaningful communication and interaction, Pac-Man provides us with a world where one doesn't have to interact or communicate at all—where all the messiness and loneliness of being separate individuals in a world full of other people can disappear, where we can at last conquer our alienation by devouring everything that we could potentially feel alienated from. And this is the triumph of the video cannibal: transcendence through absorption. But the problem is, once we clear every last labyrinth of pellets, ghosts and cherries, we emerge, stunned, into the labyrinth of real life, a social life full of people and problems that we can't deal with by eating.

This social "leftover" is another way of explaining the eyes of the ghosts. No matter how solipsistic our fantasy worlds become, they are haunted by the look of the other person, by the lurking suspicion that, no matter how all-consuming the fantasy, there are still people outside us, watching, devouring us with their gazes, invalidating our dreams of total transcendence with their judgments. The knock on the door while you're masturbating, the concerned look on your mother's face that you try to ignore as she crosses the room while you butcher pixilated prostitutes, the eyes of the ghosts: these are the troublesome remainders. These are what must be "cleared" by compulsive play, what must be finally devoured in the cannibalistic fantasy space where solipsism and addiction meet.

However, while Pac-Man implicitly promises to turn the gamer into a kind of Supreme Eater, it also converts him into food. It was, after all, a pizza with a slice missing that inspired Pac-Man's design. Pac-Man is food that devours. He is our food in that we absorb his identity during playtime and use it to munch our way through hours of gaming fun. We also consume Pac-Man by wearing him on our t-shirts, trading him on our trading cards, and literally eating (i.e. chewing and swallowing) him in our cereal and mac & cheese. But this "food" (and I think we could extend the metaphor to video games in general) in turn consumes us. We get to fantasize that we're gulping everything into ourselves all the while our time and consciousness are actually being converted into money and incorporated into some video game corporation. In fact, this whole solipsistic cannibal fantasy—the one that lets me eat and eat until I'm the only person in the world—is totally dependent on about a billion other people having the same fantasy, converting their time, energy and hard-earned quarters into serious corporate capital.

And now when I take a break from my video game-fantasy land and emerge into that labyrinth of real life that I mentioned before, I encounter other pac-addicts who wear the t-shirts, swing the lunchboxes and trade the cards, and make me realize that, not only am I not the only person in the world, but I'm not terribly unique either. My status as both eater and eaten stares me in the face, and it hits me that I'm just another flapping mouth and pair of ghostly eyes.

STRANGERS IN THE NIGHT

Gary Allen

Vampires and the Meaning of Blood

We mean several different things when we use the word "vampire." There is, of course, the Hollywood variety—an undead being that must consume the blood of the living to "live." We will come back to them, shortly.

The Masai's primary source of protein is the blood of their cattle. They do not kill their animals; they merely "tap" them periodically. Marco Polo described the Tartars habit of drinking their horses' blood—squirted hot into their mouths from opened arteries.

We do not call them "vampires," in spite of the literal truth of the designation. We may think it barbaric, but we do not see such bloodletting as monstrous or evil.

We consume blood puddings, blood or black sausages—such as the classic French *Boudin Noir* or German *Blutwurst*—with only the slightest trace of *frisson* or, perhaps, the relish of flaunting a slightly faded taboo. Mandarin Hot and Sour Soup, thickened with cornstarch today, originally derived its velvet viscosity from duck's blood. The *ragoûts* of game known as *Civets* in France, or the similar Jugged Hare in England, always include a thickening touch of blood, often ox blood. Thai beef noodle soup, *Kuaitiao Neua*, also contains the offal and blood of cows. Americans tend to be a bit squeamish when it comes to "variety meats" or blood. It's not that there is some primitive or demonic presence in these foods—they're simply less nice than "real" meat.

A Small Aside about Meat

There is a popular misconception about the eating of rare meat: many people believe that the *jus* that is so desirable with prime rib, for example, consists of the blood of the animal. It is not blood, because all the blood is carefully drained away during the butchering process. The carcasses of slaughtered animals do not produce more blood after that final fact. The *jus* is actually intracellular fluids that are released either through the process of slicing the roast, or literally squeezed out of the cells by the contraction of muscle fibers exposed to high heat. It may be that this misconception is perpetuated, not just by ignorance of the biological facts, but by other desires. When we consume something that we *call* blood, we play at being wild. It is akin to our urge to go camping or to eat a picnic lunch: we temporarily pretend to throw aside our civilized façade and live like our "wild" ancestors. That is why the smell of burned flesh is the heart of these expeditions to our common past. Our charcoal grills are the descendants of the sacrificial altars of the ancients.

Leeches, biting insects, and vampire bats are unnerving, but innocent, creatures. We may refer to them as "blood-suckers" or "vampires," but the casual way we do so is humorous because it is clear that we don't really think of them as "vampires." While we may not be anxious to provide such creatures with sustenance at our expense, we do not attribute sinister motives to their feeding. Yes, they do try to drink our blood—but they do so without indulging in the magical or mental corollaries of the act. It is not the blood-sucking, itself, that repels us. It is some ancillary aspect of the act that frightens and intrigues us.

We commonly suck our own blood, and that of those closest to us, when we accidentally cut ourselves, and we don't always spit it out, as we do when treating snakebite. We think nothing of it. It is such an ordinary occurrence that when the cinematic Dracula is suddenly interested in a cut on Jonathan Harker's finger, we are yanked into another level of awareness. The offer to help with the injury is clearly not going to be beneficial to Harker. What is so sinister about it?

Blood as a Symbol for Life Essence
What is it that makes the *idea* of blood drinking so much more threatening than the act itself?

Primitive man, even before the invention of formal rituals, saw a connection between blood and life. Reay Tannahill describes the hypothetical development of this relationship in *Flesh and Blood*. Our ancient ancestors

> *...knew that life was uncertain and sometimes short, that death was inevitable and sometimes abrupt. Every time he set out for the hunt he was aware that some day, perhaps today, the end would come with a slash and an outpouring of blood. It is not difficult to understand why... he should have come to the conclusion not merely that blood was essential to life, but that it was the essence of life itself. ...[there is] the long-standing belief that if flesh and blood had independent potency, they could be regarded as transferable assets. ...For one man to absorb the blood of another (living or dead) was equivalent to absorbing part of his essence, his force, his nature.*

Farb and Armelagos, in writing about food taboos, described the origin of Kosher slaughtering procedures with respect to some of the ancient attitudes toward blood: the spirit, or life essence, of all animals is in their blood, so when they are slaughtered, their blood must be drained so that spirit can return to the earth.

The Shariah, or Sacred Law of Islam, spells out, in occasionally gruesome detail, what may or may not be eaten. Many of these laws, like rules of Kashrut spelled out in *Leviticus*, concern the slaughtering process and, specifically, the flow of blood from the slaughtered animal. Only if all laws are obeyed can the flesh be transformed from *haraam* (forbidden) to *halaal* (permitted). The four "veins" of the neck (carotid artery, esophagus, jugular vein and trachea) must be severed while the animal is alive, and the blood must gush.

Christians drink the blood of Christ, symbolically, at Communion without experiencing violent revulsion —although, for children, first communion and the mystery of blood are often more primitively visceral, less cerebral. Two old women from Cevennes reminisced about the time in parochial school when,

> *"The nuns had told us, If you chew the host, you'll get a mouthful of blood! A friend asked, And if we bite it do we die? After that we were all jittery when we had this host in our mouths! And then it was hard to swallow, it sat in our stomachs, and we were afraid of vomiting it because it was a mortal sin."*

So blood is not just blood—it is not just a bodily fluid. It stands for all the things that allow us to distinguish the quick from the dead. Think of what we mean when we describe someone as "hot-blooded" or "cold-blooded." We have very clear, very emotionally charged, ideas about this subject.

When we are wounded—especially when we defend family, loved ones, or country... our blood is "spilled." We understand, implicitly, that we are merely vessels that hold this precious substance—and that the value of the vessel is insignificant without its contents. Empty bottles, especially bottles that once held alcoholic beverages, are often called "dead soldiers," "dead marines," "dead men," or "tramps." Before removing an empty glass, a bartender will sometimes ask *"is this dead?"* In Italy, a waiter might ask—before removing an empty wine bottle—*"il soldato e morto, eh?"* (this soldier is dead, yes?). "Dead soldier" is also a slang term for a penis that has just ejaculated—reinforcing the notion that an empty vessel is worthless.

Consider what we mean when we describe someone as "bloodless." We're implying that such people are not fully human—that something is missing from them, something intangible but important. They lack that indispensable complex of attributes we call the "soul."

It does not matter whether we consider such notions psychologically, anthropologically or magically—blood is, symbolically, a very important substance.

Similarly, drinking has important symbolic characteristics. Wolfgang Schivelbusch, in *Tastes of Paradise*, addressed the act of drinking in terms of its magical function. All liquids are symbolic blood, which in turn are the symbolic life, "vital fluid," or soul of a plant, an animal or even a location (water is sometimes perceived as the lifeblood of a place). When we drink, we assimilate the soul of someone or something else—and our own soul is diminished proportionately. Classically, a drunken person is not filled with his or her own soul, but with that of the wine, or of the wine god, Dionysus. Incidentally, there are many slang terms for intoxication that imply that one has been demoted to the level of a foodstuff. As examples, a drunk may be "baked," "boiled," "cooked" "corned," "creamed," "fried" or "pickled." In France, to have had too much *vin* is "etre beurré"—to be buttered.

When we drink, we capture one of the trickiest forms of matter. Fluids are shapeless, ever-moving, ever-changing. The metaphors we use to get a grip on our most elusive concepts are invariably constructed of liquids. Thoreau, for example, wrote, "Time is but the stream I go a-fishing in. I drink at it; but while I drink I see the sandy bottom and detect how shallow it is. Its thin current slides away, but eternity remains."

To drink is to contain, to become a vessel for something vague, but powerful—and the vessel is nothing, except when it is filled, its value determined by the liquid within.

Blood as Fuel for the Dead

Blood is the sacred liquid that distinguishes animate from inanimate matter. If we believe that the dead have consciousness, and we believe that they are envious of the living, and if blood is the thing that characterizes the quick, then it follows that the dead must crave it. Neanderthal and Cro Magnon graves are often found stained with red ocher—a practice seen among Stone Age cultures to this day. It is intended to add the color, if not the actual magical properties, of blood to the pallid dead. Skulls are often decorated with this sanguine mineral.

In Book 11 of *The Odyssey*, Homer described Odysseus' descent into Erebos to consult with the shade of blind seer, Teirêsias. He sacrificed two sheep, collecting their blood in a pit. Immediately, the dead began to gather around the pit, trying to taste the blood.

The Countess Báthory used to bathe in, and occasionally drink, the blood of young virgins—in the hope that their youth and beauty would rejuvenate her own aging skin. The weird logic of her accounting was inescapable: if it is blood that distinguishes the living from the dead, and the young and beautiful are more alive than the old and ugly, why not move that important commodity from one side of the ledger to the other? No doubt Báthory felt herself growing more beautiful with every victim—and it is safe to assume that her unwilling blood donors grew considerably less vibrant as the transfer was effected.

Certainly, that's what happens when vampires drink our blood. That's bad enough, but we are troubled by something else. We become empty vessels. We lose not only our lives, but that which makes us "us." Leeches and insects may drink our blood, but vampires drink deeper—they drink our metaphorical blood. Even worse than the loss of this precious substance—the magical fluid that animates and ennobles us—is the fact that the vampire is not ennobled by it.

Think about those mindless revenants, the zombie-like creatures in *Night of the Living Dead*. They attack and kill the living as a source of energy only. They literally eat to live—but what sort of quality does such "life" hold? The undead creature, be it vampire or zombie, is a base vessel that cannot be improved by our loss, only maintained at the same horrid level.

It is the meaninglessness of our loss that horrifies us.

When we use the expression "He's bleeding me dry," or "bleeding me white," we are layering metaphor within metaphor. We are substituting money (or the absence of it) for blood, and blood, as we have seen, symbolizes life essence. When we complain about these modern-day "blood-suckers," we are upset that we are having our substance, our worth, our very life, drained away.

Dracula

When we think of vampires, the most often conjured image is that of the suave, dark, continental stranger—created by Bram Stoker, and portrayed by Bela Lugosi. Most of us know that Stoker's Count Dracula was based on a real person, still known as "Dracul" in Romania, but as Vlad Tepes or Vlad the Impaler, everywhere else. Most of us are vaguely aware that he was a monster of some sort, but are uncertain about the connection between the modern idea of Dracula and the historical figure. As it turns out, there are a number of curious connections between the two Draculas.

Vlad Tepes lived from 1431-1476. He was, at three different times, Prince of Wallachia, a small country bounded by Transylvania on the north, Bulgaria on the south, Moldavia to the east, and Serbia to the west. He was, to use modern terms, a patriotic terrorist who was fairly successful in his own land—but whose fame was spread, internationally, through the use of new communications media: the printing press. His enemies were able to tell the world of his terrible atrocities because the press allowed pamphlets to be spread cheaply across Europe.

One of these pamphlets, from Germany, contains the best-known, and nearly contemporary, picture of Vlad. The woodcut shows him seated at an outdoor table set with food and drink. Behind him, to his left, stands a small forest of stakes, bearing seven or eight impaled victims. Before him, a servant is using a large hatchet to disjoint several other victims. The ground is littered with hands and feet, and a severed head is simmering in a cauldron in the lower left corner.

The implication of the print is that Vlad was feasting on his victims—'though, to be perfectly honest, the draftsmanship does not allow us to identify the entree sitting on the trencher before him. There are stories about Vlad eating human flesh and drinking human blood, but there doesn't seem to be any evidence that he actually did so.

Where, you might ask, is the drinking of blood? How did this renaissance warlord, terrifying as he was, become the stuff of classic horror, the symbol of undead—and undying—evil that we know today?

The credit for this evolution of the character of Dracula can be laid firmly at the feet of Bram Stoker—but the *idea* of vampires was, of course, much older. Tannahill explains:

> *Among the vampire's ancestors were the demons of many lands. There were the* vetalas *of Vedic India, evil spirits who took up their abode in corpses, and the* ghuls *or ghouls of Arabic folklore, spectres who feasted on the living. There were the* lamiae *of ancient Greece and Rome, nebulous witches who sucked blood, and the* strigæ, *ghostly but lascivious, who raped people or drank their blood with cheerful impartiality… But the majority of vampire-like stories featured either straightforward ghosts with a liking for blood, or "living ghouls," who were merely human beings with depraved tastes.*

Beginning in the middle ages, stories containing monsters that more nearly resemble our idea of vampires began to appear. A ruling by the Eastern Orthodox church claimed that the bodies of the excommunicated could not decay until they received absolution. Therefore, in areas of much contact between followers of the Eastern and Roman churches, the faithful were quite willing to believe that the cemeteries were filled with "viable" bodies, ready to climb out of their graves to haunt the living. The region where Vlad had lived was just such a place.

Vampirism was used exactly as cannibalism has been used—as a means of defining and dehumanizing The Other. Eating habits are used to define The Other—and the vampire's narrowly cannibalistic diet is perfect for the task—so vampire stories, over time, became part of the folk mythology of the region.

Literary vampires followed a somewhat different track, one that will seem oddly modern to us. The story of how Mary Wollstonecraft Shelley came to write *Frankenstein* has been told a million times, but rarely do we hear of her competitors' stories.

In 1816, Mary Shelley, her step-sister Claire, Percy Bysshe Shelley, Lord Byron, and Byron's personal physician—John

Polidori—were vacationing in Geneva, Switzerland. To pass the time, they decided to write ghost stories. *Frankenstein* was a result of this little contest. Byron wrote the outlines of a story about a vampire—but never bothered to complete it. The two classic "movie monsters" were created at the same time, in the same place.

John Polidori took Byron's idea and turned it into a story called "The Vampyre." It was not well-received at first, but as a result of some confusion over the story's provenance, Goethe and other European literati took up the theme. By the time Bram Stoker came on the literary scene, some sixty years later, vampire stories were *everywhere*. There were vampire plays in many of the London theaters of Stoker's day, at a time when the most famous serial killer of all time, Jack the Ripper, stalked his victims through the London smoke. The time was ripe for Stoker to write a vampire story of his own. Raymond T. McNally and Radu Florescu described the beginnings of the Dracula saga:

> *Around 1890, he met with a Hungarian scholar, Professor Arminius Vambery, whose travel talks were already known to him. ...Bram was impressed by the professor's stories about Dracula the impaler.*
>
> *...the British Museum had purchased one of the German pamphlets... which related horror tales about Dracula. ...Although the pamphlet does not describe Dracula as a "wampyr," it does call him a cruel tyrant and a* wütrich, *an old German term for "berserker" or, more literally, "bloodthirsty monster."*

Stoker tied all these disparate influences together, seasoned it with a uniquely Victorian horror/fascination with sexuality, and created the archetypal exocannibal for his times (Dracula was, for Victorian England, what Hannibal Lecter is for us: strange, cultured, smooth, terrifying and irresistibly seductive). Over time, the notion of the vampire has evolved to survive in our ever-changing geography of fears.

Destroying the Vampire

In the movies, the vampire is sometimes "killed" by exposure to sunlight. Vampires (and ogres) are destroyed by sunlight because their cannibalistic natures can only survive in the dark recesses of our ancient heritage. They are undone by exposure—by revelation, in the Christian sense of the word, or, in psychological terms, by transference from the unconscious to the conscious mind. While that was a significant part of the stories, in the past— such a method of dispatch is too passive for modern tastes.

In the United States, there was a vampire-like hysteria that ended at the beginning of the twentieth century. Bodies of suspected vampires were exhumed and mutilated in various ways. Sometimes the blood of the cadaver was drunk. At other times, the heart was burned and the ashes were stirred into a drink for the vampire-killers. In 1898, in Rhode Island, the body of a young woman was exhumed because other members of her family were afflicted with tuberculosis. It was believed that their increasing weakness was due to her nocturnal depredations. Her heart was cut out, burned and fed to her tubercular siblings. In all of these cases, the ingestion of vampire parts was supposed to confer immunity to future attacks by the undead. Most of the folk remedies for an infestation of vampires are missing what we now consider an essential ingredient: the sharp stick through the heart. Why is that?

The vampires of tradition are not like the Dracula of the movies. Dracula, as we know him, is a pastiche of historical figure and folk nightmares. The fictional monster can only be dispatched with the preferred technique of the historical model. Thanks to Stoker, Dracula will always be destroyed, as Vlad destroyed, by impaling on a wooden stake.

The Confusion of Meanings for Blood

Today, Goth clubs are frequented by young—mostly urban—disaffected souls who fancy themselves as vampires. Indeed, some of them actually drink each other's blood. The mythic and magical qualities of the vampire have been transformed into commodities by a culture that is too hip to admit that it could harbor such *bêtes noirs* in its collective unconscious.

While it appears that the vampire has been rendered safely camp by post-modernist sensibilities, it has merely changed its form. Today, the vampire has assumed a modern, scientifically recognizable form, while subtly lurking—in classic Gothic fashion—in the remaining dark corners of the pre-modern psyche. As Nina Auerbach noted, "every age embraces the vampire it needs."

The vampire still gorges himself on our metaphorical blood, but the metaphor itself has undergone metamorphosis. AIDS and other blood-borne diseases—such as the horrible Ebola virus—have changed our notions about blood itself.

The magical substance that was, for thousands of years, a metaphor for life has become a vector for death. And not merely death, but relentless, implacable, destruction of life, carried out by flesh-consuming monsters, invisible cannibals that devour us from within. We are hosts to microscopic aliens, like the creature in the movie, that eat everything but our pathetic skeleton.

In old stories, when the vampire crept up behind us—his image did not appear in the mirror. Today's vampires tend to lurk *inside* us—we stare at the mirror, in horror, as our own faces slowly morph into the very image of death, our blood slowly drains away, and our skulls emerge from the still-living, but decomposing flesh of our faces.

RECIPES

Irish Coffee

Ply J.P. Donleavy with whiskey until he has passed out (indicating that the proper level of marination has been achieved). Place in large barrel, top off with more whiskey, and age until the next wake or other celebration occurs. Strain a generous jigger into hot sweetened coffee cups—enough for all the patrons of all the pubs in Dublin that the author used to frequent (you'll need lots of coffee). Top with whipped cream of British nobility.

Gary Allen

Benedictine Cordial

Carefully withdraw the still-beating heart of a young monk and plunge it into a cask containing brandy and an assortment of bitter herbs. Allow mixture to steep for a fortnight. Strain the resulting liquid, discarding all earthly remains, and sweeten with simple syrup until beatified.

Gary Allen

THE KITCHEN STAFF

Ken Albala, *co-editor*
Ken Albala is Professor of European history at the University of the Pacific. His books about food include *Eating Right in the Renaissance* (University of California Press, 2002), *The Banquet: Dining in the Great Courts of Late Renaissance Europe*. His latest book is *Beans: A History* (Berg, 2007). He co-edited, with Gary Allen, *The Business of Food: Encyclopedia of the Food and Drink Industries* (Greenwood Press, 2007).

Gary Allen, *co-editor*
Gary Allen is constantly writing and editing books about food—his essay here is adapted from one of these works-in-progress: *How to Serve Man: On Cannibalism, Sex, Sacrifice and the Nature of Eating*. He also writes articles for magazines, symposia and websites (he's Food History Editor at *Leitesculinaria.com;* and Webmaster for the Association for the Study of Food and Society's site, food-culture.org, as well his own site, *On the Table*). His most recent book is *The Herbalist in the Kitchen* (University of Illinois Press, 2007). In his spare time he's an adjunct professor at Empire State College.

For reasons that remain unclear to him, some people are reluctant to eat the home-cooked meals he prepares in New York's Hudson Valley.

The contributors to this book represent a diverse group of individuals, some representing various academic disciplines—which was expected—but practitioners of the arts, journalism, law, and medicine are also here. Some might find it a little un-nerving to know that—considering our topic—one contributor describes herself as "a Registered Nutritional Consultant Practitioner."

Harry Brown

Harry Brown's studies in Native American and colonial culture have led him to become interested in stories of cannibals, real and imagined. In his teaching and writing, he has further explored white cannibals like the Essex survivors, individuals forced by circumstance to transgress taboo and then, returning to their communities, to face the social and psychological consequences. His book, *Injun Joe's Ghost*, appeared in 2004. He teaches American literature and writing at DePauw University, in Indiana.

Janet Clarkson

Janet Clarkson is interested in culinary and medical history, but more interested in eating and drinking. Unfortunately she has to earn a living—hence she actually works as a medical practitioner in Brisbane, Australia, where she finds it advantageous to describe ancient remedies to her patients, thus making them more grateful for their own treatment.

She would really rather be cooking pies than doing almost anything else.

Lisa Cooperman

Lisa Cooperman is an artist in Stockton, California and Curator of Education at the Haggin Museum. Food packaging materials play a frequent role in her sculptural work, which is exhibited nationally. Her illustrations for "Gastrabulary: a Future Terminology of Eating," written by Ken Albala, appeared in *Gastronomica*. She also illustrated *Cooking in Europe: 1250-1650* and *Cooking in America: 1840-1945*, both from Greenwood Press.

Their story, "Fat Chance," is their second collaboration.

Dennis DiClaudio

Dennis DiClaudio is a writer and editor living in Philadelphia. His stories, poems, essays and plays have been published in *One Story*, *Exquisite Corpse*, *Post Road*, *Pindeldyboz*, *Bullfight*, *Eyeshot*, *Konundrum Engine Literary Review*, *Yankee Pot Roast* and

McSweeney's Internet Tendency, among other journals. They involve facial deformations, incestual urges, scarification and a child who is born as only a liver. His first book, *The Hypochondriac's Guide to Horrible Diseases That You Probably Already Have*, was published by Bloomsbury USA in 2005. A good friend, and literary mentor, once gave him the following piece of writing advice: "Remember the body."

This advice was possibly taken too much to heart.

Terence FitzSimons

A former stipendary magistrate in Rhodesia/Zimbabwe Terence FitzSimons has, in his time, had to deal with a variety of strange and wonderful court cases. He has encountered witchcraft, wizardry, and necromancy—and, indirectly, cannibalism. Now resident in Australia, Terence teaches sociology at the University of Ballarat, Victoria. All in all, he finds this a (slightly) less stressful undertaking than sitting in criminal court.

Ellen Fried

Ellen J. Fried is a lawyer, weekend sailor, and food enthusiast with a Master's Degree in Food Studies. She became intrigued with legal issues surrounding infamous cases of cannibalism on the high seas, but soon turned her focus to the depiction of cannibalism as *haute cuisine*. This led, in turn, to an exploration of the ad industry's use of cannibalism motifs to sell everything from chewing gum in the 1930s to cigarettes and blue jeans in the 1990s.

She has concluded that, when it comes to advertising and cannibalism, absolutely nothing is sacred or taboo.

John Kohagen

John Axel Kohagen, though currently living in Bloomington, MN, will always be a small town Iowan boy at heart. He currently teaches literature for a small college. From growing up around farms and livestock, to spending a lot of time with chefs and chefs-to-be at work, he's well aware that good food often comes with devilish stories.

He lives with two wonderful cats and a wife who is kind enough to tolerate his oddities.

K. A. Laity

K. A. Laity is the resident medievalist of the English department at the University of Houston-Downtown. On a campus surrounded by bayous filled with snakes, carp and alligators, her thoughts often take a morbid turn as she struggles to persuade students to share her love of Anglo-Saxon texts. When not writing scholarly essays, she turns her energies to writing fiction inspired by things from the mythic to the gothic, for which she won the 2005 Eureka Short Story Fellowship. Just to prove that she is safe for children, her novel *Pelzmantel: A Medieval Tale* was nominated for the 2003 Aesop Prize and the International Reading Association's Children's Book Award.

Mike Lee

Mike Lee was born in Winnipeg, Manitoba. He first became a student of the intersection between cannibalism and culture under the tutelage of loving grandmothers who baked him gingerbread men and called him things like "sweetie pie." He took his M.A. in English at the University of Western Ontario where he did work on Oswald de Andrade's *Cannibalist Manifesto*. He is currently in the doctoral program at McGill University, examining the relationship between cannibalism and vegetarianism in nineteenth-century England. His poems have appeared in *Incunabula* and *The Collective Consciousness*.

Laurel Massé

Laurel Massé is an internationally-renowned vocalist (and a founding member of *Manhattan Transfer*) who has spent much of her life traveling. She has always appreciated the sensuous pleasures of good food. She tasted her first artichoke at eight, and her first order of escargots at ten; since then she has been fascinated by what people will or absolutely will not eat, and by the fact that food and the sharing of food lie at the heart of our most ancient and sacred rituals.

Alice Mills

Alice Mills is associate professor of literature at the University of Ballarat, in Australia. She has a scholarly interest in the grotesque and abject and has edited a collection of essays on these subjects and another on the unspeakable. Her story, "Roast Fallopian Tubes," was inspired by a visit to Vietnam where she did indeed go to a restaurant with roast fallopian tubes on the menu… the rest is fiction.

Pedro Malard Monteiro

Pedro Malard Monteiro has eaten pork today. He is currently digesting his repast on the lovely hills of Nova Lima, in Brazil. He is said to have been born on the other side of those hills, in Belo Horizonte, in 1971, though accounts, and the reliability of sources, vary widely. He started cannibalizing the English language in 1989 and felt all the better for it. He finds English as delicious as his international friends, who come from all continents, with the sorry exception of Antarctica. He earned a PhD in English from SUNY-Albany, where he acquired the habit of accepting strange dinner invitations, mainly from Europeans and Asians, whom he misses a great deal. He has no known allergies to any edible living organism. His literary diet includes nutritious delicacies such as António Lobo Antunes, Lydia Davis, Graham Swift, and Julio Cortázar.

Richard O'Corozine

Richard O'Corozine, a painter from grade school to the present, exhibited in NYC (SoHo and 57th St.) in the 1970s and 80s. He has been writing for the last 20 years—mostly plays. *The Carcass* was performed at STU Theatre in Krakow, Poland (2002-3), and was performed, Fall 2006, in Hamburg, Germany. *Ba-Ba: the Car* performed at Apple Blossom at MASC in Poughkeepsie, NY (1990); *Etna* performed by Apple

Blossom at MASC (1991); and performed by Passion Place at MASC (1994).

O'Corozine's play, *The Echo*, was performed by Passion Place at MASC (1993), and by the Edinburgh University Psychology Department at Edinburgh Fringe Festival, Scotland (1995). It is based on a real-life cannibal—Albert Fentress—who, in 1979, killed and partially ate one of his students.

Jeri Quinzio

Jeri Quinzio is freelance food writer, a former advertising copywriter, and author of a recipe book called *Ice Cream: The Ultimate in Cold Comfort* (Brick Tower Press, 2007). She was a contributor to *The Oxford Encyclopedia of American Food and Drink*, *Scribner's Encyclopedia of Food and Culture*, and *Culinary Biographies*.

Along with her ice cream, she especially likes to eat bones of the dead.

Suzanne Rindell

S. E. Rindell is a writer and poet from San Francisco, and has recently completed her first novel. Her work has appeared in *The Georgetown Review*, *Sulphur River Literary Review*, and *The Texas Review*. She is an active member of *l'Alliance Française*, likes to paint in greyscale, and spends much of her free time looking for new hiking trails in her native California.

Gene Santoro

Gene Santoro has written about popular culture for numerous publications, and has authored five books, including *Myself When I Am Real: The Life and Music of Charles Mingus* and *Highway 61 Revisited: The Tangled Roots of American Jazz, Blues, Rock & Country Music*. "Rockefeller Rockefeller" marks Santoro's debut as a cannibal-watcher, although he once led a band called "The Alferd Packer Spoonful," and feels strongly that cannibalism, in one form or another, is an essential feature of human society.

Riva Soucie
Riva Soucie lives in Ottawa, Ontario (Canada). She is an MA Candidate in Sociology at York University and a Registered Nutritional Consultant Practitioner. She is pursuing her PhD at Carleton University in the Department of Sociology and Anthropology (where she is studying women's food work as activism). Her writing can be found in *Burnt Toast*, a national food magazine.

Six of her cuticles are currently infected.

Camilla Trinchieri
Born in Prague to an Italian diplomat father and an American mother, Camilla Trinchieri came to the U.S. when she was twelve and returned to Italy when she graduated from Barnard College. In Rome she worked in the movie industry as a dubbing producer/director with Fellini, Luchino Visconti, Lina Wertmuller and many others. She came back to New York City in 1980, married, got an MFA from the Columbia's Graduate Writing program and became an American citizen. Fascinated by the repercussions of violent death, she has published seven novels (the last four with HarperCollins) and several short stories in the mystery genre under the pseudonym of Camilla Crespi. Under her own name, she has had several non-genre pieces included in anthologies.

Tamara Watson
Tamara Watson is a poet living in Poughkeepsie, New York, home to several dozen unsuspecting dentists. Her work has appeared in a number of publications including *Poetry Now*, *Second Coming*, *Bitteroot*, *Nimrod*, *13th Moon*, *New York Quarterly*, *The Massachusetts Review*, and the *Paris Review*.

Peter "Toots" Wheat
Peter "Toots" Wheat is the *nom de plume* of a restaurant critic for a major West Coast newspaper, who—obviously—has a number of excellent reasons for keeping his identity hidden.

He is the first to confess that he thinks, and talks, entirely too much about what—or whom—he eats, usually in the form of run-on sentences. He also agrees, sadly, with Mary Pettibone Poole, who once wrote, "Alcohol is a good preservative for everything but brains."

Darius Willoughby

Darius Willoughby is the acclaimed author of scandalous short stories by night and insurance salesman by day in his hometown of Dewdrop, North Dakota. He is the recipient of the prestigious Mildred Peasley Bangtree Award for Impossible Palindromes.

Made in the USA
Coppell, TX
28 February 2022

74236999R00138